HUMANISM
AN INTRODUCTION

HUMANISM
AN INTRODUCTION

JIM HERRICK

WITH A PREFACE BY LAURIE TAYLOR

Prometheus Books

59 John Glenn Drive
Amherst, New York 14228-2197

Published 2005 by Prometheus Books

First published in Great Britain in 2003
By the Rationalist Press Association

Inquiries should be addressed to
Prometheus Books
59 John Glenn Drive
Amherst, New York 14228–2197
VOICE: 716–691–0133, ext. 207
FAX: 716–564–2711
WWW.PROMETHEUSBOOKS.COM

09 08 07 06 05   5 4 3 2 1

Library of Congress Cataloging-in-Publication Data

Herrick, Jim.
   Humanism : an introduction / Jim Herrick.
      p. cm.
   Includes bibliographical references and index.
   ISBN 1-59102-239-8 (pbk. : alk. paper)
   1. Humanism. I. Title.

B821.H47 2005
144—dc22
                                                        2004014878

Printed in the United States of America on acid-free paper

For Christopher Findlay

Contents

Acknowledgements

The following read all or parts of the manuscript and made many helpful suggestions for which I am extremely grateful:-
Christopher Findlay, Frank Jordans, David Pollock, Diana Rookledge, Jane Wynne Willson.

I am very grateful to Clifford Harper for his cover design.

Introduction

It sounded an easy way to win half-a-crown. All I had to do was to stand in the middle of the playground at my Catholic school and shout out in a voice that was loud enough to be heard by the giggling crowd of fellow fifth formers who'd come up with the bet: 'If there really is a God then I challenge him here and now to strike me dead'. But I can still recall the drumming of my heart as I slowly walked towards what I still secretly feared might be a date with destiny.

I'd brought it on myself. For the best part of a year I'd been trying to convince my school friends that there was no proper basis for the religious dogmas that we were being force fed in class. It had earned me a certain mild notoriety but I was only too well aware that my dismal failure to effect any conversions to atheism had something to do with the shallowness of my own arguments. I'd told my classmates, for example, that the idea of a virgin birth was a contradiction in terms. You simply couldn't be a virgin and have a baby. Didn't they know the facts of life? I'd also argued that the miracles of the loaves and fishes and the raising of Lazarus were really nothing more than clever conjuring tricks and even made the profoundly heretical suggestion that if Jesus was God and God was all knowing and all powerful then he surely he could have avoided his own crucifixion and gone on teaching until a ripe old age.

As I struck my pose in the middle of the playground, I made a resolution which neatly captured my adolescent moral capacity to have it both ways at the same time. If God failed to strike me dead after I'd made my challenge then I would devote myself to the task of discovering some rather better reasons for not believing in his existence.

I got my half-a-crown and kept my pledge. By the time I'd reached the sixth form I'd read enough philosophy and literature to be able to take on even the most slippery religious opponents. I might not have known all fourteen of the 'arguments leading to atheism and agnosticism' outlined by Jim Herrick in the following pages but at least I no longer needed to rest my case on playground melodramatics. When the time came for National Service I felt confident enough to write 'atheist' in the place on the form reserved for religious beliefs.

(It hardly had the effect I was hoping for. 'We don't have a box for atheists', I was told. 'We'll put you down as C of E').

It was only later in life when I came into contact with good honest sincere life-enhancing people who insisted that their morality was not derived from religion, that I realised that atheism was not enough. Not believing in God provided no basis whatsoever for knowing how to live one's life. This was the time when I began to take a serious interest in human values, in the moral resources that people drew upon when they were called upon to justify their actions. My work as a criminologist eventually led me to recognise that I did not need to rely upon the virtuous in my quest for such ethical imperatives: even the most committed delinquents and hardened criminals lived at least part of their lives in accord with a set of principles that would have found favour with the most rigorous moraliser.

In some ways I wish that as a result of all this, I could now claim to have discovered a set of moral values as substantial and prescriptive as those that were impressed upon us at school by the priests and the brothers. But in reality I relish the ambiguity about how to live one's life that results from abandoning a closed system of belief. It is this, I suppose, that makes me resistant to announcing myself as a 'humanist' or a 'rationalist'. These are labels that at times can do more to announce the foreclosure of a debate than the start of a productive argument.

Jim Herrick is thoroughly alive to this problem. His account of humanism does much to trace its historical development, its philosophical underpinnings, and its current status as an alternative to systems of religious belief. But he is always faithful to his underlying contention that 'humanism is a position which thinking individuals can reach as a personal conviction'. So, while he is always informative, he is never prescriptive. He does not stand in the middle of playground shouting out his disbelief. He opts for the more restrained and considerably more fruitful task of showing his readers that 'humanism is not the triumph of the human' but a philosophy that 'can give us hope that we may act constructively in the future and live richly in the present'.

Laurie Taylor

Humanism Outlined

Humanism is a most human philosophy of life. Its emphasis is on the human, the here-and-now, the humane. It is not a religion and it has no formal creed, though humanists have beliefs. Humanists are atheists or agnostics and do not expect an afterlife. It is essential to humanism that it brings values and meaning into life.

As we move away from the morass of the twentieth century, we can hope that humanism will be a beacon to help us through the twenty-first century. It is an approach that is neither optimistic nor pessimistic, but realistic. The nature of human behaviour in war, oppression and violence makes us pessimistic: but the human capacity to go beyond this can make us optimistic. There are issues such as changes to global climate, which may make us very pessimistic, but our human determination to act can be powered by optimism.

The word has developed since its use to describe 'renaissance humanism' to its twentieth century use to describe a belief system that calls upon reason and values to enable us to develop our lives and our societies. Sometimes adjectives are added – such as 'scientific humanism', 'ethical humanism', 'religious humanism' – but it is better without adjectives, for unity and clarity and purpose. Humanism can develop depth and meaning as a fully expressed belief system. Just as religion can be developed at a theological and a devotional level, so humanism can be developed at a philosophical and a practical level.

Humanism is a philosophy of life to be found across the world, from Oslo to Rio de Janeiro, from Manchester to Hyderabad. It may not always be openly avowed for some may be over-prudent and some may not have clearly thought out their position. Although there are humanist organisations across the world, their members are a fraction of those who hold to a humanist philosophy. While it can bring strength to be related to other humanists by belonging to a group, it is not necessary to join an organisation or follow a leader or study a particular text. Humanism is a position which thinking individuals can reach as a personal conviction and an individual way of life.

1

Humanists, although not religious, will live beside the religious, believing in freedom for religion and freedom from religion. The humanist will be unhappy about societies that give privilege to religious groups, but will not support persecution of religion. Some humanists will wish to take part in the public debate about religious beliefs, querying the dogma of the various religious systems; most humanists would not wish to undermine the religious beliefs of a neighbour whose belief helps them to get through life. And humanists will wish to work together with the religious in relieving poverty, releasing the persecuted, assisting the aged, and so on.

Humanists do not believe in miracles, though they can comprehend the sense of the miraculous. There seems no evidence that the laws of nature are suspended for a particular 'miraculous event'; but the smile of child who has been cured by antibiotics can seem miraculous. We can believe that the hidden life of a person can be revealed, but not that there is a supra-natural component to the universe likely to hit us as a revelation.

Atheism alone is not humanism – for Stalin was an atheist. Humanism is atheism/agnosticism with values. Our morality is social in origin. It comes from the way we have evolved and from our ability to see that there is general benefit if we behave well towards each other. Humanists derive their moral codes from human need. It is necessary that some of these codes may be regulated in society to deal with those who have not developed a moral sense. But the highest level of morality is developed personally as the individual moves towards an idea of personal and social goodness. Moral behaviour need not involve martyrdom or sacrifice, it is possible to develop a sense of contentment together with a sense of responsibility towards others. This is not necessarily smug self-satisfaction: there may be much struggle needed to attain personal happiness and social harmony. There will never be a perfect human or a perfect society.

Humanists believe morality stems from our situation as social animals. Our morality may affect our relations with other than human animals, but as far as we can tell they do not have moral instincts or codes: what morality controls a cat's attitude to a mouse? (Perhaps some primates have social instincts.) Morals come from our altruism – even though this is not equally developed in all people. Also the codes of behaviour in society come from our social agreements, our social construct of morals that benefit us all. Without the ability to empathise with the distress of others morality does not operate effectively. Humanists will say that a moral instinct and moral values in society are very important.

Science as a method of inquiry is of great importance to humanists. The method is perhaps as important as the results, which may – with further research – prove wrong. There are two aspects of science – the steady research to solve problems and develop new theories – and the applied use of such research in technology in the creation of new implements, the bombs, the mobile phones, the artificial heart valve. Although most scientists would wish to take a responsible attitude to the use of their research, it is the technologists and the entrepreneurs who have control of the hands-on development. We may all be unhappy with the uses towards which some science is put, but our adherence to the scientific method as a means of understanding the world is paramount.

The open and democratic society is important to humanists. The principle that all in society should be able to participate in the way it is run, from parish council and school governors to the House of Commons or the United Nations, is essential. It may not be desirable for everyone to have access to all information in society, for instance, in the public domain, how to make nerve gas, or, in the personal realm, knowledge of a terminal illness. There should be a principle of assumption of the right to know as a starting point. There will be an open discussion on how to distribute the wealth and opportunities throughout society, but humanists will tend to be concerned with justice and some measures of levelling wealth.

Sometimes humanists are caricatured as dry rationalists worshipping pure reason. But it is unreasonable to extend the use of reason to all areas. The emotions and the aesthetic sense are important for a full life. The feelings of love, of adventure, of sorrow, of hope, all contribute to a rich life. Whether in the arts or in nature the sense of beauty beyond the human demonstrates both our capacity to experience the world and also how small is the importance of each individual.

Humanism is a way to live, to give meaning to life and to find an understanding of our place in society and, indeed, the universe.

The Humanist Tradition

The tradition of humanism is a long one. It questions existing ideas and quests for new ones. People have asked what powers control our lives, what is the nature of the world about us, what is our personal potential? From the documents of ancient history to the flowering of thought in ancient Greece, from renaissance Italy to the eighteenth-century Enlightenment, from the wide developments in philosophy and science in the nineteenth century to the crystalisation of humanist ideas in the twentieth century, the humanist temper has developed through time.

In ancient thought scepticism can be found in religious documents. In one of the Upaniṣads in ancient India come the lines:

> Is Brahma the cause? Whence are we born?
> Whereby do we live, and whither do we go?
> (Śvetāśvatar Upaniṣad)

The idea of the Hindu God Brahman is questioned root and branch.

Later a Hindu school of thought known as the Cārvakā in the sixth century B.C. held that the Hindu sacred literature is false, that there is no deity, that all life is matter, that there is no immortality, that priests are of no value and that pleasure is the aim of life. 'The wise should enjoy the pleasures of the world. . .'

In the Bible it is written: 'The fool hath said in his heart: there is no god.' (Psalm 14) This is evidence that atheistic thought did exist that early. Much evidence of early humanist thought comes from the negative source of its condemnation.

In early Chinese thought Confucius (551 – 471BC) wrote: 'To give oneself earnestly to securing righteousness and justice among the people, and while respecting the gods and demons, to keep aloof from them'. This suggests that morality can still exist divorced from religion. Confucianism, although providing a religious framework, contains the seeds of humanism within it. Another world religion – Buddhism – contains a sceptical and atheistic strand.

Ancient Greece

An astonishing explosion of art, philosophy and science took place in the fifth century B.C. in Greece. At this time Greeks believed in a very wide range of gods and had a diversity of religious practice. Perhaps the comparison of the gods led to a questioning of their existence.

A group from Miletus, a Greek colony on the coast of Asia-Minor, took up the major questions. One of them was Thales (630/20 – 546/35 B.C.) who said all existence was based on water. Anaximander is thought to have written a book *On Nature* which has not survived, while a fragment from his friend Anaximines' *On Nature* remains. They set out the 'naturalistic view' that everything is based on matter and left no role for the spirit in inert or living matter.

The drama and sculpture of ancient Greece shows a preoccupation with the entirely human which was new to human culture. It is hard to imagine that the human form will ever be captured in stone so well again. The symbol of Prometheus bringing fire to the world was used by the playwright Aeschylus; Prometheus speaks of 'How I made men rational and capable of reflection, who till then were childish.'

Some Greek philosophers laid down the essential foundations of humanism. In his work *Of the Gods*, Protagoras (481 – 411 B.C.) stated 'About the gods I have no means of knowing either that they exist or that they do not exist or what they are like to look at; many things prevent my knowing – among others, the fact that they are never seen and the shortness of human life.' It was not so much that the gods were removed from the cosmos, but that they were seen as irrelevant.

Protagoras became well-known and wealthy, but he was indicted for impiety and probably drowned while trying to escape across the sea to Sicily. A most relevant quotation for humanists is: 'Man is the measure of all things, of the reality of those which are, and of the unreality of those which are not.' This is a simple statement of fact, not a proud declaration of human superiority as some commentators have suggested. He was an analytic and sceptical thinker and may have initiated the questioning dialogue as a means of seeking truth.

Socrates (469 – 399 B.C.) is renowned for his use of dialogue as a means of philosophical exploration and it is a profoundly humanist method of inquiry. His views, as recorded by Plato, (428 – 348 B.C.) are not humanist; he saw a divine order in the universe and did not endorse the open mind or the open society. But although he was not an atheist, he recognised that atheists could lead upright lives.

5

Aristotle (384 – 322 B.C.), another great philosopher of the period, disagreed with much of Plato's thought. His approach was more empirical – looking at the evidence without preconceived theories. His study of ethics is based entirely on the human. In common with many Greek philosophers, scientific research and speculation was important to him.

Perhaps the most important Greek philosopher from the humanist perspective was Epicurus (341 – 271 B.C.). He believed that the gods did not exist or at least were indifferent to humanity. His followers conversed and reflected on philosophy in his garden. He believed in the search for a contented human life. This was not lust for sensuous pleasures, but moderate pursuit of peace of mind. One of his statements is particularly characterisitic: 'Friendship goes dancing round the world proclaiming to us all to awake the praises of a happy life.' His influence in the following centuries was enormous, especially in the form of the long poem by the Roman Lucretius *On the Nature of Things*.

There was less speculative thought in Roman times, although Cicero (106 – 43 B.C.) wrote *On the Nature of the Gods*, which covers many of the arguments about the existence of deities.

The medieval period was essentially dominated by Christian thought and Christian institutions. Some questioning is to be found in diverse heretical movements and it may be that an undercurrent of critical thought has left no record save for the occasional grotesque gargoyle! Arab culture and thought during this period was considerably more developed in terms of science, art and philosophy. The philosopher Averroes (1126 – 98) born in Spain, was an original and heretical thinker, and among those who transmitted Greek thought to the thinkers of the renaissance.

The Renaissance

The renaissance began with the revival of classical learning and was underpinned by the development of city life in Italy. Like all such cultural movements it may have been fuelled by increased trade, prosperity and leisure time. Renaissance thinkers used the phrase *studia humanitatis* in referring to the study of the humanities (rhetoric, grammar, literature and philosophy) rather than humanism in the modern sense.

As with ancient Greece the blooming of human-centred arts, painting and sculpture and poetry, provided an exceptional insight into human behaviour, thought and existence. There was also an increased emphasis on the civic, in a period when the power of the city state was prevalent. Vittorina da Fletre (1378 – 1446) an educationalist at the University of Padua, wrote: 'Not everyone is called to be a lawyer, a physician, a philosopher, to live in the public eye, nor has everyone outstanding gifts of natural capacity, but all of us are created for the life of social duty, all are responsible for the personal influence which goes forth from us.' 'The life of social duty' is an important emphasis in humanism. Philosophers who challenged the prevailing catholic ideology, brought themselves into difficulties. Pompanazzi (1422 – 1525) wrote about the immortality of the soul and when he suggested that there might be nothing beyond death he found it necessary to deliberately obscure his argument to avoid the Inquisition.

Giovanni Bruno (1548 – 1600) was less prudent. He was a Dominican monk who studied science, mathematics and literature in the style of the true renaissance thinker. He defended Copernicus' view that the sun was the centre of the solar system, criticised Christian ethics, and called for religious toleration. He was arrested by the Inquisition, refused to recant, and was burned at the stake.

The criticism of the Catholic church came from the reformation as well as from sceptics. The development of print and the ability to read the Bible in one's own language enhanced the capacity for independent thought about religion. Wars of religion led to a 'plague on both your houses' mentality.

An essayist who particularly deplored religious strife and intolerance was Michel Montaigne (1533 – 1592). He was active as a magistrate in Bordeaux, but later retired to his tower, where he penned a series of the finest essays ever written. Inscribed on the beam of his room were the words 'Homo sum, humani a me nihil alienum puto' (I am a man. I consider nothing human to be alien to me. – Terence).

Another essayist, Francis Bacon (1561 – 1626) stood at the end of the renaissance and the beginning of the age of science. He was not an atheist and his essay 'Of Atheism' has often been quoted: 'a little philosophy inclineth a man's mind to atheism, but depth in philosophy bringeth man's mind about to religion'. Nevertheless, his understanding of the scientific method, in particular the importance of experiment, and his survey of knowledge gave the lead to the scientific age and the enlightenment. Scientists are not necessarily irreligious, but the search for tested knowledge rather than received knowledge affected considerably people's way of looking at things.

The Enlightenment

The eighteenth-century Enlightenment was an intellectual and active movement centering in France. Voltaire was its most towering figure. He was mathematician, poet, playwright, satirist, philosopher. In his long life (1694 – 1778) he was constantly on the move, frequently at war with various authorities, taking up cases of injustice, above all seeking fame as a writer.

A satirical piece about the monarchy put him for a short spell in the Bastille as a young man. It taught him to 'harden_myself against adversity'. Among his most famous works was the *Treaty on Toleration* (1764) which was written as a consequence of his fight to restore the reputation of the Protestant Calas family, who had been accused of murdering their son because he wanted to become a Catholic. Voltaire endorsed the principle of free speech, which includes the defence of the rights of those with whom you disagree.

His best known book is *Candide,* a brilliant satirical tale in which the naïve Candide believes all is for the best in the best of all possible worlds. This literary ploy often demonstrates the opposite, for instance, when Candide visits El Dorado:

> Candide was curious to see the priests; and asked where they were. The good old man smiled. 'My friends,' said he, 'we are all priests; the King and all the heads of families solemnly sing praises every morning, accompanied by five or six thousand musicians.' 'What! Have you no monks to teach, to dispute, to govern, to intrigue and to burn people who do not agree with them?' 'For that, we should have to become fools,' said the old man: 'here we are of the same opinion and do not understand what you mean with your monks.'

Voltaire probably retained little religious belief, while perhaps thinking belief in God was a way of keeping the people in order. Certainly he rejected Christianity utterly.

So did Diderot, who was a more explicit atheist. He had a warmth in human relations and an ardour in the tasks he set himself, which make him an attractive figure. His life's work was editing the *Encyclopaedia* – a compendium of knowledge with many subversive articles hidden in unexpected places. During its composition his rooms were searched for manuscripts 'contrary to Religion, and the State or Morals'; he was arrested and briefly imprisoned. He wrote in his *Philosophical Thoughts* that 'scepticism is the first step towards truth'. The *Encyclopaedia* was certainly full of scepticism. Before completion the *Encyclopaedia* was banned and had to be completed secretly. But it was a mighty contribution to eighteenth-century thought.

Among his many other works were *Rameau's Nephew* and *D'Alembert's Dream.* Both are witty dialogues, the first concerned with the arguments between a hedonist and a moralist, the second with the nature of scientific materialism. D'Alembert was a mathematician who assisted Diderot on the *Encyclopaedia.* Another contributor was d'Holbach, who wrote many atheistical and anti-clerical pamphlets. When the British philosopher, David Hume, visited this group of *philosophes* he said that he had never met any atheists. D'Holbach replied that of the eighteen people at the table fifteen were atheists and three had not yet made up their minds.

Two British contributors to the Enlightenment were Gibbon and Hume. Gibbon in his *Decline and Fall of the Roman Empire* removed the role of God from the course of history. He also wrote a famous chapter on the rise of Christianity under the Roman Empire in which he suggested that Christians, by refusing to acknowledge the emperor or to take part in national festivals, brought their persecution upon themselves.

David Hume was a philosopher and historian with a benign temperament and brilliant mind. His major work *An Enquiry concerning Human Understanding* contained the chapter 'Of Miracles' which has been very influential. His posthumously published *Dialogue on Natural Religion* incisively portrays the arguments about the existence of God, with the strongest arguments coming from the sceptic.

The French revolution in 1789 has been said to be influenced by the *philosophes*, but they were not revolutionaries. The accusation that atheism and irreligion led to the Terror following the revolution is hardly true since it was influenced more by Rousseau and theism than by freethinkers. The *philosophe* Condorcet became a victim of the terror, committing suicide while in prison to avoid the guillotine. In extremity he wrote his *Historical Sketch of the Progress of the Human Spirit*. His ability to write about human rights and natural dignity and human progress at this point in history speaks of the power of the eighteenth-century Enlightenment.

Radical and counter-religious ideas were developing in Britain. The idealistic founder of the Co-operative Movement, Robert Owen, abandoned 'all belief in every religion' but replaced it by a 'spirit of universal charity'. The poet Shelley, as a student, wrote a pamphlet with James Hogg, *The Necessity of Atheism*, which he reprinted as a note to his long poem *Queen Mab*. Although of aristocratic origins he was profoundly radical and wrote an outraged poem, *The Mask of Anarchy* in response to the slaughter of demonstrators in favour of electoral reform, known as the Peterloo massacres (1819).

The utilitarians were distinct precursors of the humanist philosophy. The catchphrase 'the greatest happiness of the greatest number' as an ethical aim is an oversimplification, but it places the moral realm within the purely human. Bentham towards the end of his life wrote *Analysis of the Influence of Natural Religion on the Temporal Happiness of Mankind* (1822) in which he described religion as irrational, possible to explain by the naturalistic approach, and damaging to society. He was not especially a negative thinker since he believed so strongly in education as a source of improvement for society.

John Stuart Mill, whose father had been a friend of Bentham, after an intense education in Benthamite principles, came to think that utilitarian principles were limited. Two of his most influential works were *On Liberty* and (together with his wife Harriet Taylor) *The Subjection of Women* and contained a defence of free speech and of the case for changing the position of women in society. A man who also pleaded for the rights of women – and atheists, working people and Indians – was Charles Bradlaugh, the MP for Northampton from 1880 to 1891. He had great difficulty in taking his seat in parliament because it was argued that the oath sworn on the bible would not be binding on an atheist. He later successfully proposed the right of affirmation for non-believers.

The ideas of Darwin on the evolution of species had enormous influence and made it possible to question Christian ideas of the Creation. Thomas Huxley, known as 'Darwin's Bulldog', did much to publicise and clarify his ideas. Huxley coined the word 'agnostic' to describe someone who is neither atheist nor theist, but who feels the answer to this question is unknowable. (*a- gnosis* without knowledge) In later life he became very concerned with morality and education. Scientific advance was a key aspect of the rejection of religion in the nineteenth and to a lesser extent the twentieth century. (Many leading Christians today no longer see science and religion as contradictory forces.)

The novelists George Eliot and Thomas Hardy were influential humanists. Hardy's vision was bleak, depicting individuals in an impersonal universe, without religion to comfort them. In the twentieth century many novelists have had a humanist outlook, for instance, E. M. Forster, John Fowles, and Brian Moore. Mary Ann Evans, as she was before choosing her nom de plume of George Eliot, translated two German works before becoming a novelist: D. M. Strauss's *The Life of Jesus* and L. A. Feuerbach's *The Essence of Christianity*. The spread of biblical criticism from German scholars was another important factor in the critique of religion. Today most Christians accept the historical context of the Bible and do not take it literally, something which has removed much of the need for freethought biblical criticism. The word 'humanism', as used in the sense of a philosophy of life, originates in German writings on education at the beginning of the nineteenth century. The first use of the word 'humanism' appears to be in 1808 by the Bavarian educationist, Friedrich Immanual Niethammer, in his book *The Quarrel of Philanthropism and Humanism in the Theory of Educational Instruction of Our Time.*

Marx in a famous phrase described religion as 'the opium of the people' at a time when opium was widely taken and widely believed to be a comfort. His theories of the inevitable stages of historical progress, taken up by communists, would be likely to be rejected by humanists as too deterministic.

In the twentieth century humanism moved into the mainstream and was found in numerous writers and currents of thought. Freud's ideas supported the view that religion could be best understood by an appreciation of the unconscious mind: he wrote a book in which his views on religion are expressed in the title *The Future of an Illusion.* The scientist Julian Huxley, who followed his grandfather in researching and propounding the theory of evolution, was the first director of UNESCO and the first President of the International Humanist and Ethical Union; he believed in what he called 'religion without revelation'. The philosopher and peace campaigner Bertrand Russell is one of the most remarkable humanists of the twentieth century. His essay entitled 'Why I am not a Christian' is justly famous. He wrote in his autobiography, looking back on a long life, that despite the ferocity of twentieth century wars and the cruelty stemming from twentieth century dictators, he still retained his personal vision – 'to care for what is noble, for what is beautiful, for what is gentle: to allow moments of insight to give wisdom at more mundane times' and 'to see in my imagination the society that is to be created, where individuals grow freely, and where hate and greed and envy die because there is nothing to nourish them'. Those in the humanist tradition would share these ideals.

Humanism, Philosophy, God and the Afterlife

> It is wrong always, everywhere, and for anyone,
> to believe anything upon insufficient evidence.
> W. K. Clifford

Humanism is a questioning, questing philosophy of life. It is linked to those philosophical ideas which lead to scepticism, empiricism and realism. Philosophy tended to become extremely specialised in the twentieth century and it is not necessary to follow it all to identify yourself as a humanist. Earlier philosophers such as Aristotle, Plato, or David Hume took on the large questions of the purpose of life, how life is to be lived, and whether there is a meaning behind it all.

Scepticism – the continual doubting of all we are told or all that we see – is fundamental to the humanist outlook. This is not a know-nothing stance which leads to paralysis, but an alert attention to what we see and think. There are no 'Keep Off' signs for sceptics: religion, science, philosophy itself are all open to question.

Complete sceptics will ask how they can know what they see around them. We receive knowledge of the external world by our senses, our sight, our hearing, our touch. How reliable are they? To spend every hour, every minute wondering whether what you see or hear is real or illusory would make the daily process of living impossible. So we live by a working assumption that what we perceive is really there. But the complete sceptic has a questioning of all as his or her bottom line. We think of the medallion of Montaigne, which had inscribed on one side: 'What do I know' and on the other 'All that is certain is that nothing is certain'.

A leading sceptic among the philosophers of ancient Greece was Pyrrho (c360 – 270BC). A sceptical tendency is common in Greek thought as exhibited by the question and answer technique of the Socratic method. Pyrrho's thinking led him to follow no particular school of thought or religion. He is said to have lived a life of great calmness, secure in his knowledge of his lack of knowledge.

Scepticism is one of the foundations of humanism but is not sufficient in itself. Complete scepticism could lead to a nihilistic belief in nothing or a cynical belief that nothing is of value. Humanism goes beyond this to put forward positive aspects of being alive and living with others. Scepticism is an approach that is valuable in science and which can be applied to questions about the existence of god, the value of religion, the possibility of an afterlife, and the extent to which miracles can be accepted.

Humanists find their scepticism about the claims of religion leads them to become atheists or agnostics. In fact, since we are born with no beliefs, we cannot be a 'born again' humanist. It is not possible to prove or disprove the existence of a god or gods. To be an atheist is to be without a concept of god (a-theism from the Greek *a* meaning without and *theism* meaning belief in a god.) To be an agnostic is to be without knowledge of a conceivable god, usually used to describe the position of 'I don't know' in relation to the god hypothesis.

Among the arguments leading to atheism or agnosticism are:

1) It is not possible to believe in all the different gods which have been put forward from different religions. If they cannot all be true, then can any of them be true?

2) God is always described from the eye of the beholder. The kind of god we believe in is determined by where and in what society we live. A cockroach would believe in a cockroach-type god.

3) If god is omnipotent and all-good, how can disasters exist in the world? Voltaire argued this very strongly after an earthquake in Lisbon (1755) caused death and devastation.

4) If god is all-good and he created men and women in his own image (male or female?) how come that people can behave so abominably?

5) Does god have a beginning or an end? If god had a beginning from what did it emerge? To describe god as the originator of the universe is not an answer to the question where did everything start, for we need to know the origin of the originator.

6) Does the evidence of the world indicate that it was created by a designer? Is there a first cause? The evidence is that life can emerge from chemical-electrical conditions without a 'maker'. We know that planets have their origins as break-away parts of the sun, that the solar system is a part of a much vaster universe. We cannot tell where the universe originated from, but there is now some speculative evidence that this universe is not the only

one. It also seems likely that there are many other life forms on other planets. To argue for a designer is merely to give a word to a process partly known and partly unknown.

7) Is god's purpose visible in the universe? We know of no purpose in the universe. Certainly there is no evidence that the universe's purpose leads up to humankind. We may yet prove to be a transient species on earth. The process of evolution is leading to greater complexity and adaptability but not towards any specific ends.

8) If god is all-powerful, of what use can human worship be to it? Surely, the puny prayers of humankind would not be of much value to a god?

9) Does not all goodness stem from god? How otherwise could we know good or be good? To say god is good is a tautology. Why not accept that there is goodness in the human species? That it is a type of action or a state of being entirely consistent with our evolution as a species and as individuals. There is evidence that altruism, acting on behalf of another without personal gain, has developed during the evolutionary process improving the survival of the species.

10) Are we not impressed by the fact that all societies seem to have worshipped some kind of a god? This may be so – although there are enormous differences in the kinds of gods and in the ways in which they are supposed to act in human lives. The fact that something has been believed for centuries does not make it true. It was believed for many centuries that the world was flat and that the sun went round the earth.

11) Implicit in the concept of an omniscient, benevolent deity is the existence of its counterpart – evil, or its personification – the devil. If god is alleged to have created everything, he or she must have created the devil. But why? Or is it impossible to create humans without an element of evil? It might be possible that god and the devil were simultaneous, separate creations – in which case the universe is an arena in which god, or his incarnation, Jesus, fight it out eternally. This is regarded by Christians as a heresy. The many questions about the nature of evil serve to undermine the concept of a deity.

12) Many religious people argue that their belief in god is derived from personal experience. God has appeared to, or spoken to them. These are subjective experiences which it is difficult to convey to those who have not experienced them. To the outsider they might be regarded as hallucination or imagination. Undoubtedly some people do have intense experiences, which seem to put them in touch with a divine force. But

these cannot be used to prove the existence of anything any more than someone might try to prove the existence of their dreams. Humanists might accept that an intense experience seeming to link with the transcendent might take place, might even happen to humanists. But this is only a demonstration of the human faculty for intense experiences, not of an experience of god.

13) One of the most important philosophical positions on atheism and theism has been put forward by the philosopher Antony Flew, in his essay 'The Presumption of Atheism'. He argues that theists have always claimed that it is up to atheists to prove their atheism. On the contrary, he contends, it is up to theists to prove their theism. In arguing about the existence of the Loch Ness monster you start with a presumption that it is inherently unlikely that it should exist and move to the need to prove the existence of some such Nessie. In the same way in debating the existence of God, there should be a presumption of atheism.

14) A final point in the discussion about the existence of god: some twentieth century theologians have put forward a conception of god very different from the traditional one. They argue that god is 'the ultimate', 'the ground of our being', 'that which underlies the energy in the universe'. These concepts are vague, but some who find it impossible to believe in a traditional god (for the kinds of reason given above) find them helpful. It is difficult to see of what value is a notion of god as an impersonal force (as found in some Hindu beliefs) underlying everything. Many priests do in fact come close to this position, because they have thought a great deal about the inadequacies of the argument for a god, but they do not explain it when they are preaching.

These arguments relating to the existence of god are not exhaustive and demonstrate the extent to which humans have weighed up the matter since the beginning of thought. It is quite possible to be a humanist without spending a great deal of time on the philosophy of deism or atheism, even though it is a key part of the humanist position. Many will live their lives without any idea of god taking part in their existence, just as many religious believers follow their beliefs without much philosophical thought about them. The unexamined life may find ways of living a fulfilled and worthwhile existence without philosophy.

Nevertheless it is in the nature of humanists that they tend to have a sceptical undercurrent to their lives.

Some religious people argue that humanists must feel impoverished without god and have a dry, cold picture of the universe. On the contrary, humanists are able to stand in awe of the universe, to be astounded by the beauty of nature, to be astonished by the extraordinariness of human potential – but none of this needs a concept of god, let alone the worship of such a being.

How far does a belief that god underlies our life really help? It can create a sense of guilt, helplessness and fear as well as comfort. Many humanists see their lack of belief in a god as a liberation (if they are moving from theism to atheism) or a sure understanding (if they have always been atheists). The great Enlightenment writer, Diderot, wrote:

> I was lost in a great forest at night, and had only a tiny light to guide me. A stranger came and said to me, 'My friend, put out your candle, so that you will find your way better'. That person was a theologian.

Many people link a belief in a god with the expectation of an afterlife. Humanists do not see the evidence or follow the arguments for this. In some religions (notably Hinduism) this is extended to a concept of a pre-life, as part of a chain of reincarnation. For humanists the evidence for this too, is doubtful.

Some people believe in the complete resurrection of the body – the original personality still embodied within it. Alternatively there might be the survival of a soul – the non-physical part of the person – with personality intact or without individuality preserved. The idea of immortality as the creation of a lasting imprint through children, by artistic productions, by original ideas, by the memories in surviving friends, which humanists accept, is not the kind of immortality which the great religions talk about.

The desire for an afterlife is understandable. The desire for everlasting survival may even have an evolutionary base. More likely is the impetus that comes from the fear of personal extinction. But are our lives any the better for hoping for a hereafter, especially if there is a presumed reward or punishment for the sum of our life's activities. The fear of eternal punishment, much used in Christianity until quite recently, is just as likely to cause confusion and inertia as good living. It is notable that vivid depictions of hell do not play a great part in modern religion, though the carrot of heaven is happily held before the believer. It has been useful for rulers and priests to encourage the idea of heaven or hell as a means of controlling people. Would so many have gone to war if it were not inculcated into them that they would receive an eternal reward? Would suicide bombers go ahead without the prospect of heaven?

There are central biological and philosophical problems to the idea of an afterlife. The biology of physical decay is incontrovertible. It is obvious that after the body's systems stop operating the corpse will rapidly decompose.

Personally, I am quite content to think that my body becomes some sort of universal compost wherein my atoms are reconstituted in a myriad of other ways. In some cases the body decays before death to an extent that makes life painful and insufferable. In some even more tragic cases the mind disappears before the body dies, with forms of dementia. Is it possible to believe in the reconstruction of the body or retention of the mind in the face of these experiences?

Philosophers and scientists have debated greatly about the question of the relationship between the mind and the body. Recent scientific research has found how parts of the brain are related to a specific feeling or thought. There seems to be a chemical-electrical activity closely related to all mental activity. It is quite apparent that the chemicals in alcohol, tranquillisers or tobacco change our state of mind. Thought and mental concepts appear to us to have their own life, but they need the activity of the brain to exist at all. Mind and body may be so interlinked that it is impossible for thought to exist without brain activity.

We are not fully human beings without the society within which we exist. Our sociable nature is the essence of our being. How far could that be reproduced in any afterlife?

There have been some claims for survival of perceptions in so-called 'after death' experiences. These should more accurately be called 'close to death experiences', since the recall of the experience is itself evidence that death has not taken place. There are some similarities in the experiences recounted: rushing through a long tunnel, the mind floating above the body, the appearance of a guide or relative. The most likely explanation of these experiences is the withdrawal of oxygen from the brain, creating the same experiences for many. Lack of oxygen is known to cause hallucinations. Of course, these experiences should be taken seriously – but remember that until they really become 'after death' experiences they give us no new knowledge of the hereafter.

Another kind of evidence for the after life often cited is that of the contact with the 'spirits' on 'the other side'. Spiritualism is based on this belief. This proposes a spirit, usually incorporeal, but sometimes seen as a ghost. The trouble is that these communications only take place to those who want to see or hear them. The spirits are notoriously shy of sceptics. If there is survival of the mind, as coherent, meaningful, interesting thought on the other side then there is small evidence of it in the messages that come through. Nevertheless, it is reasonable to continue research into these phenomena even if they at present yield so little.

Reincarnation is a form of after-life attractive to some people especially within Hinduism and Buddhism. But how can there be sufficient bodies for people to be reincarnated into with the growing generation of souls? If the purpose is to improve oneself from life to life, how can this be done when the knowledge of past behaviour has vanished. The occasional ' memories' of a former life, sometimes under hypnosis, seem all to be too close to the romantic, historical novel to really convince.

It is a fact of nature that we must make way for the next generation. The ground would be cramped by the crush of humans if there were no death. The thought of immortality on earth is alarming. Even with the prospect of eternal good health, which is impossible to imagine, how could we continue to remain fresh to life over several hundred years? In Swift's *Gulliver's Travels* there is a voyage to a country, Luggnagg, in which a small number of people are born with a spot on their forehead, which means they will not die. This is thought to be the greatest calamity that can befall anyone.

Humanists look positively at our mortality. It is a fact of existence which we must come to terms with. It can ensure that we take full advantage of the one life we do have. We turn from the feeling that 'At my back 1 always hear, Time's winged chariot drawing near' to a determination to make something of our life with those around us.

Although the rich life which we can have (some of the time!) may seem little short of miraculous, humanists do not believe in miracles based on the supernatural. By miracles I mean those events which are contrary to the laws of nature as we understand them. Traditional Christianity relied greatly on miracles as evidence of God's work around us. In fact, since most miracles are presented as divine intervention on the face of the earth, the position of atheist or agnostic already weakens the likelihood of accepting miracles. To call an event miraculous is only to describe the event in a different way and not really to offer an explanation. The position of the humanist is not prayerful thanks to the Almighty, but to consider the need for further investigation. God is not an explanation for miracles any more than miracles are an explanation for God.

Miraculous powers are often thought to demonstrate the power and truth of religion. David Hume, one of the great philosophers of the Enlightenment, wrote that when someone told him that he saw a dead man restored to life, he was forced to consider the probabilities whether the person was deceived or whether the fact had happened. In weighing up these alternatives he would have to decide which was the greater miracle. 'If the falsehood of his testimony would be more miraculous than the event which he relates; then, and not till then, can he pretend to command my belief or opinion'.

Many miracles must have naturalistic explanations. In cures from illness, it is necessary to take into account the psychological aspect of the person where mind and body are inextricably linked. In miraculous appearances of supernatural figures, for instance the Virgin Mary, it must be remembered that people and especially adolescent children can be very vulnerable to hallucinations. There may yet remain incidents and reports which have no ordinary explanation. Humanists will wish such cases to be thoroughly investigated. They may accept that, either there may be possibilities within the workings of nature which we do not fully understand, or that it is as satisfactory to accept the 'don't know' position as to proffer an explanation which it is impossible to substantiate.

It is worth noting that the account of a miracle often involves personal interpretation. The one person who is not killed in a motorway pile-up attributes his or her salvation to a miracle; but the dozen or so dead are merely the detritus of the workings of nature.

A humanist will accept the wonders of nature, the depths of human love, the rapture of poetry as more than sufficient for the loss of miracles.

Humanism is a realistic and pragmatic philosophy. With its concentration on the here-and-now it contrasts with 'idealism' and metaphysics as the base for living. 'Pragmatism' is one of the philosophical approaches which is closest to humanism. It is based on a scepticism towards our knowledge of the world and the decision to take what is valuable for our actions in the world as the 'working truth'. It has some similarities to utilitarianism, which sought, at its simplest, to base action on the 'greatest good of the greatest number'.

It is contrasted with ideology – a collection of beliefs and values held for a specific group of people and a particular programme of action. Lenin wrote that 'practice alone can serve as real proof' – showing himself to have a pragmatic foundation for what became communist ideology. Humanists are cautious of all-embracing solutions or teachings, preferring to ground each question and idea on the practical, the particular and the personal. A philosopher who called himself a humanist was F.S.C. Schiller – a pragmatist, influenced by the father of pragmatism, C.S. Peirce. Some have commented that the fact that pragmatism was started and pursued particularly in the USA is consistent with a practical, materialist, get-ahead approach to life.

Another school of philosophy important for humanism was logical positivism. This outlook was preoccupied with linguistic empiricism. These philosophers examined sentences relating to metaphysical ideas, such as 'There is a God', and came to the conclusion that the sentence had no meaning. A.J. Ayer, who was one of this group, was active in the humanist movement. The philosophy of this group has faded, since the analysis of all statements to the level that they become meaningless reduces our understanding of both language and the world.

Although humanists are often interested in philosophy, it is not in the least necessary for them to become expert philosophers. Nevertheless. since Plato and Aristotle philosophers have dealt with the broad questions of what is the world and what meaning there is in a human life in a way which humanists find of great interest. There is no humanist Bible or Koran, no creed or dogma, but within the philosophic tradition humanists may find stimulus for their questing and questioning approach to life.

Humanism and Morality

Can you be good without god? According to many people this question challenges all non-believers and according to humanists a positive answer to this question is a key to their beliefs. Humanists believe in god with a double 'o'. Unlike nihilists or even some extreme libertarians, humanists would acknowledge the need for a moral sense, a social conscience and the necessity to consider others.

The loss of a supernatural world is famously seen by Dostoevsky as a loss of values and a loss of moral capacity:

> If you were to destroy in mankind the belief in immortality, not only love but every living force maintaining the life of the world would be at once dried up. Moreover, nothing then would be immoral, everything would be permissible, even cannibalism. *(The Brothers Karamazov)*

'Everything would be permissible'. That is the fear and the temptation. How do humanists come to terms with the anti-social as well as the social instincts of human beings?

Morality arises because humans are essentially social animals. An individual alone on a desert island would not need to behave morally, except perhaps to avoid damaging the island for potential others, or, rather more arguably, not to pollute the island's environment for the sake of its flora and fauna. A foetus is potentially but not fully human. In those rare cases where babies have been brought up outside a social environment – for instance by a group of wolves – the being does not acquire social instincts and abilities, having difficulty even with speech and awareness of other people. The social nature of humans creates the need for morality, not from a god but from the nature of human self-responsibility and social inter-relations.

Is altruism a natural instinct? There is evidence that some of the higher animals, especially the primates, display altruism – that is behaving for others and the community sometimes to one's own disadvantage. We may have evolved genetic characteristics which make our existence social in nature and which allow us mutual cooperation as well as hate-filled conflict. Evolution is driven by the survival of the fittest and altruistic societies will survive better. The evidence of the development of moral behaviour within our evolution is still somewhat speculative and the discovery of a gene for cooperative behaviour is yet to come and the origin of such behaviour likely to be more complex than one gene. Nevertheless, it seems probable that moral behaviour is part of our nature and that we can acquire a moral sense as we develop from infancy to adulthood.

Scientists have argued (especially Matt Ridley in *The Origins of Virtue*, 1996) that we are the most social of species and our sociability has evolved. Evolutionary biology can show how co-operative instincts arise. Indeed this living in a co-operative inter-active way is one of the most striking characteristics of human beings. We know that other creatures – ants, deer, wolves – are also strongly social.

To develop a moral sense may require the genetic potential and the appropriate nurturing. The conscience may be the internalised voice of the parent telling us what to do and not to do. We probably respond much better to the example of moral awareness on the part of parents and others than from a list of commandments. We surely develop a deeper moral awareness from encouragement and self-sufficiency than from a fear of god. The response to returned human love can be stronger than to an imagined heavenly afterlife.

Morality can be learned in the family, in the school and within the community. Religions have tended to offer a carrot and stick approach to morality – heavenly reward or hellish punishment and in the more short term, the pleasure or displeasure of a god, who can be prayed to or confessed to for forgiveness or offered a sacrifice for appeasement. The phrase 'Vengeance is mine, saith the Lord' is from the Bible, but vengeance is no part of morality, indeed it may be part of the strong emotion which needs to be controlled by a moral person. Fear is not a good ground for moral actions.

The stick and carrot, the fear and favour, approach is inadequate for both a divine and a human parent. Rule-based and sanction-driven morality is not the best approach to parental caring or moral education. Once the parent has gone or the theistic belief disintegrated, the morality based on outside injunctions will slip away and the adult be left without moral direction. Moral education or civics education should have an important place in the school curriculum. It is far more valuable than teaching youngsters to pray. Moral education should offer young people the opportunity to explore their feelings for others, to appreciate that they would not like being treated in certain ways by other people. This can best be done by role play and discussion rather than being given a list of 'dos' and 'don'ts'. Much morality is 'caught rather than taught'. The ethos of a school also is very important: is there consideration for all members of the school community? Are children given an opportunity to express their views about how the school is run? Although there has been much research and discussion of moral education it is not widely found in our schools, while an Act of Worship is compulsory.

What moral acts do moral sensitivities lead us toward and away from? For all the thinking and writing of millennia of philosophers, there is a widely agreed principle which underlies all morality. It was known as the Golden Rule by the ancient Greeks: do unto others as you would they would do unto you. Or modified into: don't do unto others what you wouldn't want done to you. The two versions indicate the difference between a positive (do good) attittude to morality or a negative one (don't do harm). This principle of reciprocity is at the heart of morality. If you don't want others to mug you – don't mug others, and so on. There are difficulties: reciprocity between entirely unequal people – the man or woman who has nothing to steal may not feel reciprocity towards the rich person she or he steals from because they cannot pay for the basic necessities of life. It may be difficult for a professor to empathise with a complete illiterate or vice versa (but not impossible). Despite some limitations the Golden Rule is of paramount importance. There is a broad agreement across the religious and non-religious as to what are sometimes called 'the moral decencies' of life: although morality is not a prescription of ideals, general qualities are agreed to be part of the outlook of a moral person: honesty, integrity, kindness, love of one's family and friends, generosity, forgivingness. At the heart of a person's ability to so act must be self-autonomy and self-respect. Parents and teachers must pay attention to this: it is very difficult to care for others if you have no care for yourself.

There are qualities which religious teachers think important, but which humanists have no room for: love of god, praying for others, self-denial and asceticism. Humanists will also not think in terms of absolutes – there may be an ideal towards which we can approach, but there is no absolute rule or general principle which can guide us in all circumstances. For humanists morality is a human construct underpinned by our biological development.

The existence of human societies in relative peace within themselves is based upon an assumed but unstated contract between all the members of society. Such an implicit agreement between all societies across the world is much more tenuous as is seen by the history of warfare in the twentieth century and such an unstated agreement may be seen to break down with the actions of terrorists in the twenty-first century. This supposed contract is only a metaphor for that social glue which binds us together. We agree to such a contract implicitly because 'the life of man [is] solitary, poor, nasty, brutish and short'(Hobbes), and we want to ameliorate that struggle between individuals serving their own desires rather than consideration of the desire of others.

The unstated agreement to act morally between each other is comparable to agreeing on a Highway Code for use of drivers on the road. It is accepted by drivers because of a realisation of the disaster it would be for everyone to follow their own inclination. These are only conventions and not writ in the sky; some countries have different speed limits, some have a different agreement on which side of the road to drive. Not everyone drives considerately, for instance someone who has spent too long in the pub may disobey the law – but the general consensus is that such law should be obeyed. Occasionally people will think the law should be obeyed according to the situation rather than the rule; for instance, to cross a red light in the middle of the night when there is obviously no other car around. The existence of such a code cannot prevent road rage, just as the existence of a law on homicide cannot prevent murder. But it is a useful guide. The Highway Code is unlike much humanist morality in that it is a list of rules, whereas much morality is more complex and depends upon the situation, the people involved, and attitudes of those involved.

The law of the land is an elaborate and highly sanctioned code. It is agreed by representatives of society, but these may be privileged members of the community and it is possible to hold moral objections to some of the laws of the country. One may be a conscientious objector to fighting in a war: it is necessary to take the legal consequences, but it is a quite moral position – more carefully thought out probably than the position of most of the military's actions. One may take exception to the blasphemy law defending Christian beliefs – and this may be as reasonable and moral a position as that of those who wish to uphold religious belief in a society.

A key aspect of morality is the consequences of a person's actions. This leads to what is sometimes called 'situationist ethics'. The acceptability of an action varies according to the situation. To take an obvious example – to kill someone during a bank robbery, or during a war, or during a road accident will all be regarded as entirely different acts because of the situations. Even telling the truth – and the reliability and honesty of one's interchanges is regarded as a touchstone of morality – can vary according to the situation. A doctor is regularly faced with the situation of whether to tell a patient that they have a terminal illness. Although a humanist would veer towards telling the truth, believing that people have the right to base their feelings and opinions on accurate information, there can be a case for withholding medical information, it depends so much on the person and the situation. It might even be considered that theft of food on the part of someone starving is very different from theft of valuables by a professional burglar. To learn how to consider the consequences of your actions should be one of the important parts of moral education. In considering consequences it is important to get full and accurate information. In that sense morality is empirical and not based on absolutes.

In a number of situations where ethical thought is needed it would be seen that reliable knowledge and judgement of the consequences are extremely important. Is suicide ever justified? Can the decision to have an abortion be a moral one? Is a homosexual relationship potentially as moral as a heterosexual one? Should an adopted child be told the truth about his or her parentage? And so on.

Within the moral maze, we can in fact usually recognise what we consider to be a moral person or a moral action. There would be wide agreement if a group of people were examined as to what was moral. A person of integrity and kindness would be likely to be recognised as such in their own community. There is indeed a consensus – and it may be uncomfortable to be outside it. But another precept of humanist behaviour is to allow for diversity within a community, so that each person may follow the dictum found in *Hamlet* – 'to thine own self be true'.

What are good and evil from a humanist perspective? The idea of evil is a powerful one. It has been seen by some as a force within the world with its own energy and direction – sometimes personified as the 'devil and all his works'. Certain actions seem to stand out as indisputably evil: genocide, whether in the mass murder of Jews by the Nazis or more recently the waves of killing in Cambodia and Rwanda or Kosovo. This violence shocks by its scale, but the domestic assault of a child or the sudden death of a friend also appals us. It is hard to wrap our minds around such behaviour, even though most of us may harbour deep in our unconscious the potential for acts of evil.

To a humanist evil is not an objective force, it is a capacity, perhaps a perversion of our potential, a maldevelopment of the individual or a failure of a group of individuals. The actions of a psychopath – who has no ability to empathise with others or to envisage the consequence of his or her actions – may be due to a genetic malformation or to a childhood without any love or care to learn from. It may be due to mental illness or alcohol addiction. But psychopaths are rare.

It is the slow accumulation of absence of concern and failure of perception that more often leads to evil. Is there a demonic force that is more than malformation, that is undermining human social behaviour? It seems not. It is more an absence than a presence. To the humanist evil should not be romanticised: it is simply an accumulation of anti-social behaviour and a failure of the will to do good.

Can goodness also be seen as an independent force in the universe? Philosophers have been concerned with the quest for the good and the good life. Humanists are more preoccupied with the good life than with 'goodness' as an entity. It is worth remembering that to do good is very difficult and the attempt often results in unintended distress. The thought of 'being done good to' may not be inviting.

Is there a positive goodness that we can be infused by? Probably not. But there are exemplars and examples of good people and good behaviour which we do not have difficulty in recognising. Goodness may be found in all walks of life; indeed, it is almost a cliché to point out that it may be found as often in a road sweeper as a bank manager, in a school teacher as often as in a bishop. Goodness may be as much intuitive as intellectual and may be found as much in the unexamined life as in the thought-ridden intellectual.

The concepts of 'good' and 'evil' are conglomerates of accumulated behaviour and attitudes. There is no supernatural 'all-good' or 'all-bad'. The difference between Stalin and a child-abuser is one of scale not of kind. The Faustian metaphor of selling one's soul to the devil has non-literal meaning: some people do slowly abandon their social instincts and enter a downward spiral into darkness and cruelty. Humanists who have a model of the rational, autonomous individual often underestimate the power of lust and cruelty within the human psyche. Such powerful forces are within us not outside us.

What do humanists who seek goodness and the good life want? Is this just an absence of the anti-social, or is there an active force within us propelling us to estimable deeds. Are there humanist saints? Certainly there are humanists we can very much admire, for instance, Diderot or Marie Curie, or Nansen. They are not perfect, but they do demonstrate humanist virtues and humanist ideals. They have a powerful urge to help others and improve the world.

How far can we agree on what we want of society and individuals? Well the fact that we can easily find people we admire and detest is indicative of the consensus of moral certainties that is to be found within all societies. The aim of creating 'the greatest happiness of the greatest number' is often used: it comes from Jeremy Bentham's theory of utilitarianism. The theory was modified by John Stuart Mill and has been qualified by recent philosophers.

One difficulty of utilitarianism is that it takes no account of the different values of different components of happiness – is enjoyment of a Mozart opera to be compared with pleasure in the latest pop song? How is the short term pleasure of a bottle of wine to be compared with the long term pleasure of seeing a child develop from infancy to maturity? An action supposedly for the good of the whole of society may cause appalling consequences to a minority – for instance the atomic bombs dropped at Hiroshima and Nagasaki at the end of the Second World War may be argued to have been for the greatest worldwide benefit of rapidly ending the war, despite appalling consequences for the victims of the bombs. The calculation of the greatest happiness of the greatest number misses out the individual qualities, such as passion for justice, courage, artistic brilliance, generosity.

Nevertheless, the utilitarian principle is of value in its indication that virtue is essentially social. This is the starting point of a humanist approach to morality. All human beings are interdependent: even a total recluse lives with an imagined 'other' in the mind. Although humanists do not have a written set of moral rules, and do not believe in absolute good or evil, they are very conscious of an ethical dimension to life. They have principles to guide them and ideals to aspire towards.

5

Humanism and Religion

Humanists believe in freedom of and freedom from religion. They wish an end to religious power and religious control and religious privilege, but they accept the right of the religious to practise their beliefs and to operate their institutions. There are occasions when humanists wish to co-operate with religious people, as, perhaps, in social work such as helping the homeless. But they will retain the right to argue critically and publicly about religion – just as the religious should maintain the right to debate critically and publicly about humanism. Religious tolerance does not mean absence of disagreement, but agreeing to a society where the non-religious and the religious have equal rights. Humanists would argue for the rights of the religious in countries where they are persecuted, but they would want to be free from the imposition of religion by the state and media and free from the pressure of religion on their daily lives.

Humanism is not to be defined merely in opposition to religion, rather it is a response to the natural world, to the nature of humankind, to a cultural and historical tradition, to an emotional and intellectual understanding of humanity. Reaction to what may be perceived as the anti-social and untruthful aspects of religion may impel some into humanism. Those who have had strong religious beliefs and taken part in a strongly controlled religious group may react strongly against it. Macaulay said that Gibbon in *The Decline and Fall of the Roman Empire* wrote of Christianity like a man who had been personally injured: some ex-religious people behave with the hostility of the wounded, but for many that is only a phase.

Humanists will argue about how far it is worth spending time and energy criticising religion. Certainly, there is a case for public debate – otherwise the arguments would go by default. Humanists are ready to hold their position in the media, at schools and in university study and discussion, but they would not try to undermine the faith of a neighbour or relative to whom it provides some solace. Many would see the critique of religion as a clearing of the ground to build upon, just as early humans cut down trees in a forest before growing food. (Forest clearance is not a very good idea these days!) There was a time when critics of religion thought that it would steadily wither away and eventually disappear like the belief that the earth is flat. Bradlaugh in considering 'Humanity's Gain from Unbelief' presented a picture of slow decay:

> None sees a religion die; dead religions are like dead languages and obsolete customs: the decay is long and – like the glacier march – is perceptible only to the careful watcher by comparison over long periods.

Bradlaugh's vision of a religion-free and happier society has not arrived; although religion plays a much smaller part in western societies than it did 100 years ago, it is arguable that people are no happier, that there has been no steady progress.

Karl Marx was another who thought religion would disappear as society changed for the better. For all his wrong-headedness, he was right that religion is essentially social in origin. His vision seems hugely misguided, when we think of the persecution of the religious (and some humanists) and the repression and cruelty of communist societies. Humanists supported the struggle of the scientist and humanist Sakharov for human rights in communist dictatorships. Humanists recognised this included the right of the religious to practise their faith. In the post-communist Russian regime religions are thriving, demonstrating perhaps that ignoring religion is much more successful than persecution in bringing about its decline. Now in Russia the larger religions such as the Orthodox Church are trying to ban the newer ones such as Jehovah's Witnesses or Mormons – an example of how religions often do not love one another.

It is not easy to assess the decline of religion in Western Europe. As with all statistics it depends how you define the questions and collect the figures. It is possible to look at the decline in church attendance, the extent to which polls demonstrate belief in a deity and afterlife and so on, and the extent to which society is run on broadly secular principles. The so-called 'secularisation' of society discussed by sociologists, has been much debated.

It is a mistake to imagine an idealised period of belief in which all were devout and diligent in their worship. In Britain in the Victorian era, assumed to be an extremely religious age, the Census of 1851 displayed a surprising view. In an addendum to the Census, answered voluntarily at church entrances in England, it was demonstrated that only two thirds of those entitled to attend did so and that the Church of England had only a small majority of attenders. This dented the Anglican claim to be the majority religion and the religious claim that most of the population were religious practitioners. Both in urban working areas and labouring rural areas there was a dearth of religion. Even the Census report suggested that 'secularism . . . is entertained by the masses of our working population'. (Nicolas Walter, *New Humanist,* Volume 114, no. 1, March 1999)

Recent Church of England figures of attendance have shown embarrassingly low levels of attendance and clerics are likely to admit that we live in a godless society. Belief statistics overall in Britain suggest that 10 per cent of people are affiliated to some kind of church, that about 30 per cent believe in some kind of Christianity, that about 60 per cent believe in God (which would include other religions than Christianity such Islam and Hinduism), while about 30 per cent do not believe in God or other religious concepts. The remaining 10 per cent are 'don't knows' – 'agnostic' suggests a more distinctly thought out position than 'don't know'. Other European figures are comparable. The US, however, has much higher figures for church attendance and specific Christian belief.

Decline of church attendance and religious beliefs can be seen as a cause or a consequence of the process of secularisation. The sociological term 'secularisation' is not to be confused with the specific attitude of 'secularism' held by Secularists. Secularists espouse and campaign for a separation between religion and the state and attempt to promote a view of life which assumes that this life is all and that we must rely on ourselves. (Very similar in fact to the more recent coinage of the word 'humanism'.)

Secularisation is the name given to the changes in society which have taken place in the western world in the last 150 years in which there has been a decline of the role of religion. This consists of a decline in church attendance, a decline in religious belief, a decline in the influence of religious institutions, and a decline in the individual inclination to turn to religious explanations or impulses in their life.

Many of the roles once taken on by the religious have now been adopted by secular equivalents: doctors, nurses, psychiatrists, teachers, carers. As such skills and knowledge have advanced, the role of religion in such spheres has virtually vanished. In fact, the development of a welfare state, of insurance schemes, of pension schemes, of state hospitals and universities, has done much to make people's lives secure and predictable and no longer at the mercy of god. Of course, this is not true in many parts of the world.

The replacement by the new professions of the churches from political and economic roles in society is also part of the secularisation process. The influence of the bishops on a monarch or on parliament, once a crucial matter of state, has dwindled despite the retention of the voices of 26 bishops in the House of Lords. There is an expectation that this number will be reduced and that leaders of other religions will also be given a right to a place. Popes and primates, politicians and preachers may pronounce – but do their religious views really have much direction on the development of society? In medieval times tithes and the ban on usury had an economic effect: now the economic system is entirely secular – and, indeed, the capitalist system is used to advantage by the churches. These are all factors leading to a secular society.

Humanists will be conscious of the process of secularisation; whether it is a process influenced by the humanist impulse or social change is not easy to answer, but it is within the context of secularisation that humanism today exists. Not all commentators would accept the thesis of secularisation (strongly put forward by the sociologist Bryan Wilson). They would point to the growth of new religions, the strength of Christianity in the USA, and the power of Islam in many parts of the world. A statistic from 1958 shows that 21.6 per cent of the UK population went to church while 57 per cent of the US population were church attenders; however, 61 per cent of the UK population could name the four gospels, while only 35 per cent of the US population could. (Quoted, *Religion in Secular Society* by Bryan Wilson, the New Thinker's Library, Watts & Co. 1966). This suggests that decline or retention of religious belief and churchgoing may be for other than theological reasons.

Muslims' religious observance is high and the population of Muslims is increasing.

The widest cause of secularisation may be the steady change of thinking so that there is the expectation that reason and a consideration of cause and effect will help with explanations. Supernatural power began to be removed from explanation of the processes of life or society in the seventeenth century, and although there may be a nod towards astrology or the crossed finger today, superstition is not seriously used in decision making. (Didn't President Reagan use an astrologer?) Scientific thinking, which similarly developed in the seventeenth century, has been influential in bringing this change. We now see that tornadoes and earthquakes have rational explanations in terms of climatology and seismology rather than as divine punishments. Most people when deciding whether to take a new job, embark on a divorce, or simply plan a holiday will not seek divine guidance, but rather discuss with themselves or others the issues of cause and effect. Public events – except for rare occasions such as the opening of Parliament or the Remembrance Day celebrations – are not accompanied by religious contributions. For a brief period one local council had an atheist chaplain, before deciding to abolish the post altogether.

The decline in church attendance is not new and may suggest a model of the irreligious person as a historical norm. Even the allegedly religious cave-paintings of Lascaux may have had a religious meaning for a minority and a social meaning for the majority. It may be that similarly during the Middle Ages many were sceptical, but prudentially held their counsel. In the face of evidence of lack of belief in society today, Christians tend to argue that, despite poor church attendance, many people follow Christian beliefs in their private life. This may be so – and indeed it is the 'privatisation' of religion that is particularly noticeable in the twentieth century. Some of the 'new religions' or new branches of the old religions, lay great emphasis on the personal and private: meditation, personal feelings of ecstasy, personal connection with Jesus. People operate a 'pick & mix' approach to religion. And religion is often considered a private affair – a matter of individual conscience and personal experience. This makes it less susceptible to rational thinking and much harder to contest. It is very difficult to debate with someone who says they have just had a communication with Jesus or gained an understanding of the purpose behind the universe by deep breathing.

Some twentieth century theological developments have underpinned the 'privatised' approach. The German theologian, Tillich, wrote of god as the 'ground of our being' rather than the divine figure 'up there'. John Robinson, the Bishop of Woolwich, notoriously in *Honest to God* (1963) disseminated such ideas quoting for instance Bonhoeffer's description of God as 'the "beyond" in the midst of our life'. More recently and more radically Don Cupitt and members of the Sea of Faith group have promoted the idea that it is possible to hold religious and even Christian views without any belief in God. Followers of the Sea of Faith are virtually humanist in their beliefs, but still retain some attachment to religion as something giving shape and purpose to life and some emphasis on the 'spiritual dimension'.

The psychologist Alister Hardy undertook research into religious experience. He invited the public to send him details of their own religious experience and came to the conclusion that many people who were not affiliated to any religion had religious/mystical experience. There has been much questioning of the representativeness of these self-selected providers of information about their experiences. If someone says they have experienced god, or 'ultimate reality', or universal peace it is not possible to deny this. But the real question is how do you interpret the experience. The same experience might be interpreted by one individual as an entirely human moment of insight, while another might speak of 'closeness to god': but the experience would be the same. It would be possible to argue that there is such a thing as humanist mysticism. Certainly, most humanists would accept that there is a 'spiritual' dimension to life though they might prefer not to use the word 'spiritual' since it is so overloaded with religious associations – this dimension might broadly cover the emotional, aesthetic, and meditative part of existence. There can be a desire for a break from the oppressive world of work and the pressing consumer society to a quieter period for reflection upon one's values.

Although humanists wish to recognise this part of human experience, they also want to make clear what they find unacceptable about religion. They will feel it is right to point out, for instance, what is a rational approach to religious documents, such as the Bible, or to the historical record of Christianity. Because humanism has historically operated in the West it has concentrated more attention on Christianity than, say, Islam – although this is changing with the growth of influence of Islam and Hinduism in the West.

Humanists may regard the Bible as an important document written in a particular historic period and containing much legendary material. It can also be regarded as a great collection of literary and poetical works and a source of moral precepts. What they cannot see is a document that is literally true in all parts, despite the historical accuracy of much of it. Nor is all of it by any means edifying. The books of the Bible are deeply embedded in the historical circumstances in which they arose.

The origins of the Bible are now being seen as a collection of stories handed down orally over many generations and a large area. It is much wider than a Jewish chronicle. The exodus for instance is now seen as the migration of a group of people known as the Hyksos at a time when the dynasty of Pharaohs had weakened. This is just a short indication of the changes that modern biblical scholarship is bringing about.

Other interesting facets of the Bible include the development of the concept of Yahweh, from a tribal god competing with other gods, into a monotheistic, personal god. The Psalms and the Song of Solomon are great poetry, Job and Ezekiel are of philosophical interest.

The New Testament is more important for most Christians. It is often not realised that the earliest writings of the NT are some of the letters of Paul, which do not give a clear account of Jesus. The Gospels were written 70 or more years after the death of Jesus: three of them were based on a lost document. It is possible that Jesus did not exist as a historical figure, but was an accretion of legends. Humanists do not on the whole take the extreme view that Jesus did not exist, but they see him as a fallible human. Some might see him as misguided in his political activity; others might admire his revolutionary activity and ethical teaching, although his ethics are inconsistent – you can only produce a consistent picture of Jesus' teaching by selective quotation. The survival of a belief in Jesus suggests there is considerable power to the legend or the history of this man.

The kind of delight in the contradictions of the Bible shown by earlier freethinkers is seen as irrelevant: of course there will be inconsistencies given the historical contexts in which the Bible was written. Thomas Paine in

The Age of Reason (1794/95) wrote from the perspective of a deist and was scathing about the Bible calling it a book of 'lies, wickedness and blasphemy'. He was critical of the miracles, the virgin birth and the resurrection – seeing them as all impossible and against reason. This approach is relevant to those Christians, who take the opposite view, calling every word of the Bible true – an approach known as the inerrancy of the Bible. Such people believe in the literal account of the creation and the fall of Adam and Eve. (Proponents of Creationism in the US have fought to have the Biblical creation story taught in schools beside or instead of the Darwinian theory of evolution.) But the freethinking critique of the literal interpretation of the Bible is less relevant to a Christianity that sees the stories and injunctions in their historical context and is prepared to accept an allegorical explanation of much of the Bible.

It should be noted that many theologians and clergy today are fully aware of the highly sceptical approach to the Bible – but they do not pass on their doubts to their congregations.

The Quran is less open to such textual criticism, since it apparently originates in the visions of one man. Even this document may have arrived in a more complex way than direct dictation. Its influence and the growth of the Islamic religion can also be examined in a historical way. The task of textual criticism within and without Islam has hardly been begun. (See, *Why I am Not A Muslim* by Ibn Warraq) There is no reason why any religion should not be examined critically. Of course, there is no reason why Muslims should not be given the same rights and be treated with the same dignity as any other group in society. A tendency to identify all Muslims as fundamentalist extremists is to be resisted.

The shaky record of the history of Christianity is admitted by some contemporary Christians. The former Archbishop of Canterbury, George Carey, (not a liberal) has written:

> That religions, including Christianity, have been agents of violence and oppression is a claim I am not about to contest. Part of my new book for the millennium acknowledges as much. Down the centuries, religious adherents have been guilty of serious sins of commission and omission in this regard. (*The Guardian*, 15 October 1999)

This is put more harshly in the title of the German ex-pastor Joachim Kahl's book *The Misery of Christianity: A Plea for Humanity without God* (1968). Prefixed to the book is a quote from Marx: 'The criticism of religion is the presupposition of all criticism'. It is easy to recount the ills of the Crusades, the inquisition, the persecution of heretics, the support of slavery, the persecution of scientists, the wars between Protestants and Catholics, the support for fascist regimes, the opposition to the use of contraception, the denigration of women.

However, again historical understanding is important. Christians will claim that believers were fallible human beings operating within a particular situation. Some might point to the devil (not many today) as the cause of the listed ills. They will comment on the hospitals and schools created by Christians. They will also rightly point to the wrong doings of non-religious people.

A humanist understanding of religion goes beyond a tally of good and ill. It needs to examine the nature and function of religion in society. Sociologists and anthropologists would see religion as a 'social construct', a human creation. It can be seen as an activity which draws people together in society and a body of knowledge and understanding which helps people to give meaning to their lives. To see religion as entirely functional would be seen by religious people as reducing it to a materialist phenomenon. But that is the humanist perspective. There are other ways of binding society and finding meaning in life.

Human beings have to face illness, pain, anxiety, death; they are at risk of poverty, warfare and famine. In the face of this it is not surprising that people hunger for explanations of the human condition. To define the answer to these states as god is only to shift the question one stage further away. The anthropologist Raymond Firth says that religion is not a set of truths about the divine. 'I believe there is truth in every religion. But it is a human, not a divine truth.' The human truths may contain worthwhile values about concern for others, caring for the weaker members of society, telling the truth, gaining strength from co-operation. But they are not of divine origin.

Whether religion is admired or deplored by humanists, it cannot be denied that it exists as a social phenomenon. In our secular society there has been some decline of religion – but only in parts of the world. Humanists see values and advantages in living without religion, but will not expect it to vanish in the near future.

6

Humanism and Politics

Human beings are social animals. They live in groups and societies and nations. Politics is the consequence of living together, creating some measure of order and justice to provide a framework within which we can live in freedom according to our individual desires. Politics is the process which arises out of our co-operation in complex societies. Without it we might find chaos, with too much of it we might find repression.

Politics has become associated with sleaze and corruption, with scandals about personal lives, with incessant bickering between and within political parties. It is therefore necessary to assert that politics can be an honourable pursuit, that men and women who put themselves forward for political activity may do so because they wish to help their fellows, despite the fact that the rewards, in a democracy, are not great, neither in wealth nor in esteem. Of course, there have always been those rulers who abuse their power – sometimes in the case of dictators appallingly. That is why it is necessary to have a political system with checks and balances and to encourage the humanist idea that to enter politics is to serve the common good. Those who believe that power corrupts may be sceptical of this approach, but might remember the scope for power-lust and power-wealth would be worse in a society with no government.

Humanists believe strongly that since we live together in communities we must participate in the life of the community. This may be done in many ways, but politics is one form of participation. Humanists, who believe in no afterlife and have rare satisfaction in the reclusive withdrawal from life, are committed to playing a part in society. Of course, people will vary enormously on how or whether they wish to do this. The tradition of humanism is community-minded as well as dissident. The dissidence can lead to original thought and resistance to overmighty control. The anarchist tradition of criticism of the need for any government, while it does not appeal to most humanists, is nevertheless a serious touchstone when thinking about government. Is government rule necessary at all? If so let it be the least necessity that we can manage.

The great humanist John Stuart Mill made this clear in his essay *On Liberty*

(1859) where he discusses the way society controls by physical force through legal means or by moral coercion:

> The sole end for which mankind are warranted, individually or collectively, in interfering with the liberty of action of any of their number is self protection.

This dictum may be challenged or elaborated and refined, but it is a bench mark. Modern government interferes with the liberty of action of its individuals in many more ways than at the time of J. S. Mill. In taxation, in compulsory schooling, in control of consumption of addictive substances, in owning weapons, in building without planning permission, in an absent father supporting his children, and so on. These would be defended not on the ground of self-protection of the individual, but of the general good. Since desires and aspirations vary so much some will feel restricted by these actions. But the overwhelming feeling is that all benefit from a society that is peaceable, fair and equable. Doing good to others must be embarked upon with caution since you may be offering them what they do not want, and you may be reducing their ability to create their own lives.

Humanists believe in a society that is open, democratic, just, participatory and free. This is an approach shared to some extent with those of other beliefs, but not with supporters of a theocratic state or a neo-fascist party. Rule by a religious leader or elected (initially) despot is the antithesis of humanism. Humanists have traditionally been sympathetic to the dissident tradition and have laid great emphasis on freedom of speech. It is easy for all to say that we love democracy and fairness; humanists believe that you should be actively involved in sustaining it.

The phrase 'open society' is often used by humanists to describe the social ideal for which they hope. The phrase has most famously been used by the philosopher Karl Popper in his book *The Open Society and Its Enemies* in which he examined the historical record of thought, from Plato to Marx, which he thought inimical to a free and open society. The political philosophy of Plato raises the all important question of how to create 'good' rulers. He suggested that 'Guardians' should be properly educated to rule, but there is the implication that they would rule in a paternalistic and controlling way. Shelley's phrase 'the good want [lack] power ... the powerful goodness want' gives an indication of the difficulty of gaining open and just government.

For a humanist, the phrase is used less philosophically, and more as a means of describing a society with openness at all levels, with openness of all to take part in the process of govermnent, with freedom for citizens of access to information about what is happening in society, with the opportunity of gaining wealth and the educational means to advance in society, with freedom of artistic expression. If there is doubt whether this is possible – even partially – it is worth remembering what the opposite is like. For instance, communist rule in the USSR and Eastern Europe led to disastrous poverty, large-scale imprisomnent of critics of the system (or even original artists), and curtailment of individual liberties at every level of life. A number of humanists opposed this system as did Christians. Some humanists were taken in by the aura of hope in the 20s and early 30s in the USSR – an instance of hope triumphing over reason and close observation. In some cases dissidents have become rulers – for instance, Nelson Mandela and Vaclav Havel: both of whom moved honourably from political opposition to political power, a trajectory which humanists can admire.

Both leaders had the problem of creating a more just society out of a grossly inequitable one. The struggle for justice is an essential part of politics. The American philosopher John Rawls, whose *A Theory of Justice* argues that justice is a form of fairness and relates to the distribution of goods and rights in society. His theory argues for opposition to racial, sexual and religious discrimination. He emphasises that :

> All social values – liberty and opportunity, income and wealth, and the bases of self-respect – are to be distributed equally unless an unequal distribution of any, or all, of these values is to everyone's advantage.

The legitimacy for such a society is not a god, or the rule of a king, or even the rule of a powerful clique. It is as if we construct society according to an imaginary contract that all rational citizens could have made.

Justice means that there is a fair measure of economic distribution. Those living in great poverty might see freedom of speech as an insignificant luxury. Complete equality obviously brings about lack of enterprise and aspiration, but vast inequality – on a global as well as a national scale – brings about a sense of unfairness. There is little value in 'distributive justice' if there is nothing to distribute. Politicians have argued about whether wealth creation results better from collective or individual effort, and whether the profit motive should be supported or tamed. Most humanists support a mixed economy and are concerned that both individual effort supports the public good and collective effort is valuable in important service industries.

A society in which slavery existed could not be a just one. It is a measure of improved political sensibility in the last two hundred years that no one would now regard slavery as acceptable in society. Women's equality is also now essential and also equality for ethnic minorities. Humanists would also support equality for homosexuals. Those living without society, such as the homeless, the imprisoned, or refugees should be treated generously partly because of their inherent humanity, but also because a society which maltreats even those on its edges is not a civilised one.

The remarkable Thomas Paine, who was active in the American and French revolutions, in his book *Rights of Man* (to which he would surely have added *and Women* had he been writing today) quotes the Declaration of the Rights of Man and of Citizens by the National Assembly of France. In the preamble the document states that 'considering that ignorance, neglect or contempt of human rights, are the sole causes of public misfortunes and corruptions of Government, have resolved to set forth in a solemn declaration, these natural, imprescriptible, and inalienable rights. The list of Rights then begins

I   Men are born and always continue, free and equal in respect of their rights. Civic distinctions, therefore, can be founded only on public utility.

II The end of all political associations is the preservation of the natural and imprescriptible rights of man; and these rights are Liberty, Property, Security, and the Resistance of Oppression.

Of course, many would suggest that duties are important as well as rights. And it is much easier to declare rights than to achieve them. In a pluralist society, where individuals and groups have widely differing views, it is necessary to work towards common values, where there is respect and tolerance for all views, provided they do not threaten the security of society as a whole.

One way of achieving this is a democratic system in which all feel entitled to participate. Participating in the community can start at the level of a school council, a work liaison committee or trade union, a local council. There may also be opportunities such as jury service, school governorship, as well as working for the political parties and standing for Parliament. Many humanists work voluntarily in groups such as Amnesty International or Oxfam or voluntary organisations such as the Samaritans or Citizens Advice Bureau.

In a parliamentary democracy there are a variety of means of electing representatives; whatever the system humanists would regard it as important to vote and many might work in a political party. Fascist government, such as the Nazi rule in Germany, is a failure of the political process. To be unaware of what is happening in society and to abstain from political action is, of course, a legitimate choice – but such choice on a wide scale leaves space for the misuse of power. Humanists are not automatically left or right or the third way, but will have a tendency to support Liberal or Labour politics on the grounds of their greater emphasis on justice and change. Although there are distinguished Conservative atheists, they are not usually vocal about it, not wishing to associate themselves with social changes which humanists might wish to bring about. There is a humanist parliamentary group, which is composed almost entirely of Labour politicians – and its work is hampered by lack of Conservative members.

Humanists have tended to be very active in specific lobby groups – to change the law on a single issue. Issues for which humanists have worked hard in the past have included the right of a woman to choose an abortion (difficult though that choice may be), and the decriminalisation of homosexuality. Another issue on which humanists have been campaigning more recently is that of voluntary euthanasia. Other more counter-religious issues are the removal of blasphemy law, disestablishment of the Church of England, the end to collective worship in schools, the change of charity law to remove automatic charitable status for religious groups. Giving financial support from the state to faith schools is strongly opposed.

There is no humanist party line on political issues and individuals will hope to reach their conclusions by a process of discussion, argument and rational thought. It is sometimes asked, why is there not a Humanist Party putting forward candidates for political elections. Humanists prefer to work through the existing system. If there are church schools should there not be humanist schools, if there are Christian hospices, should there not be humanist hospices? Humanists tend to prefer to push for an enlightened state system, but there will always be need for voluntary organisations. Humanists do work for the homeless, third world suffering, prison visiting, but not usually with a humanist label attached to themselves.

Some argue that the party system of politics leads to dishonesty and corruption. In India, humanists who support the ideas of M. N. Roy argue for a partyless democracy. Gora and Sarawathi Gora, the founders of the Atheist Centre in India argued for a similar break from the party system. But the trouble is that firstly, we cannot start from scratch as though we were all virgin political beings with no prior ideas and allegiances, and secondly that any group of people will start to see the development of sub-groups with similar interests and aims so that the development of parties is almost inescapable.

Humanists believe deeply in the importance of the right to speak and write and broadcast freely. They accept that they do not always themselves agree and value the process of discussion and disagreement. Whenever a few humanists are gathered together there will be sure to be a few arguments. Obedience and towing the line are not humanist virtues. The early freethinkers fought hard and were sometimes jailed in order to publish books critical of Christianity and the political situation. There should be a presumption in favour of free speech. Since no principle is absolute, there may be controversial areas where freedom of speech should be curbed: releasing information which might harm the security of the nation might be one. But even there humanists might argue that the whole system of national security, spying, and sustaining international enmities is an unhappy one. Should neo-Nazis be given the right of free speech? Perhaps one solution would be to allow fascists the right to speak, but prosecute them as soon as they incite to public disorder.

Rushdie's novel *The Satanic Verses* caused grave offence to Muslims, who responded by threatening a fatwa against him. His life has been considerably restricted by this death threat. It is to his credit that he has continued to write creatively. Should a book be banned, which no one is required to read? Should a television play be banned, when every television has an off switch? A society which constantly controls its thinkers and artists is diminished. In a mature democracy we ought to be able to cope with art and public statements which we do not like. There is a case for permitting the availability of pornography, which some might dislike intensely.

Whatever level of freedom is obtained, humanists do not believe in any Utopia. It is valuable to have a blue-print of ideals and plans for the future, but anyone embarking on the creation of the perfect society will soon end up creating a pernicious society. The best that can be hoped for, humanists would argue, is the amelioration of the worst aspects of the human lot. The attempt to develop civic virtue and the principle , expressed by Kant, that people should be treated as ends rather than means, are humanist approaches. The shift from a religious to a humanist society is indicated by the statement of the Federal Appeals Court in 1964 in New York City, in a case in which the right of a conscientious objector to give ethical rather than religious reasons for exemption from military service: 'The stern and moral voice of conscience occupies that hallowed place in the hearts and minds of the men which was traditionally reserved for the commandments of God.' (Quoted by Corliss Lamont in *The Philosophy of Humanism*, 1949)

The striving to contribute to the community as a whole is essential to the humanist vision, even though the potential conflict between different groups in society and the human lust for power should not be underestimated. The Italian novelist, Ignazio Silone in his novel *Bread and Wine* gave the words of a priest speaking to his pupil: 'No word and no gesture can be more persuasive than the life, and, if necessary, the death of a man who strives to be fair, loyal, just ... a man who shows what a man can be.' (Quoted by Khoren Arisian in 'Ethics and Humanist Imagination' from *The Humanist Alternative* edited by Paul Kurtz, 1973) The life of a humanist striving thus to be fair, loyal, just can contribute beneficially to social and political life.

7

Humanism and Science

The scientific process and the scientific world-view are essential to humanism. Although not all scientists are humanists, all humanists will consider science to be important. Previous to the theory of evolution, it was difficult to understand how life developed on earth; previous to cosmological theories about the origin of the universe it was thought necessary to provide a deistic originator. Theories of evolution and cosmology are therefore essential to humanists' understanding of the world and the universe. Humanists do not think that science can provide everything: in personal relationships, in the development of morality, in aesthetic creativity, science is not all. But in its proper place as an explanation of the functioning of the natural world it is a key part of our understanding.

The scientific process is commonly misunderstood, and schools should teach the methods scientist use, how they theorise and make observations and discoveries, as much as they should teach specific scientific facts. It is crucial to science that theories will change – indeed most scientists would like nothing better than to develop a new theory and have it accepted by the testing and debate of other scientists, by finding that facts support it, by discovering that it works in practice and by fitting it into the pattern of the laws of nature. Pseudo-science and anti-science (which is sometimes anti-humanist) can only thrive because of the lack of scientific understanding in our society. There is an eagerness among the general public to understand science, judging by the considerable number of books explaining aspects of science, by authors such as Richard Dawkins, Paul Davies, Matt Ridley, Carl Sagan and Stephen Hawking (whose *A Brief History of Time: From the Big Bang to Black Holes* was an amazing bestseller). The prose of some modern science writers is becoming as important a part of modern literature as were essays and sermons in the past. It may be wondered how widely read and understood such books are after purchase, but they testify to a hunger for understanding of the whys and wherefores of a secular universe.

The process of science does not consist of one single activity. Traditionally scientists have been seen as conducting experiments to demonstrate a theory; then further scientists repeat the experiments to confirm – or not – the theory.

This, while containing some aspects of science, is not an adequate description of the scientific process. Some theories are not testable by experiments – the theory of evolution for instance. Science, therefore consists of a range of approaches. There is the descriptive and theoretical approach: Darwin's *The Origin of Species* began in a descriptive way and then moved towards a theoretical explanation. Its acceptability as a theory is sustained by its power of explanation and by its consistency with the growing number of facts which support the theory. It is supported at every level by the findings of palaeontology, molecular biology and comparative anatomy.

Further characteristics of the scientific process are that its ideas should be self-consistent and that explanations should be capable of being linked with other branches of science. Science tends towards greater simplicity – even though the details may become more complex, the basic theory tends to remain simple. Whatever branch of science is involved the same laws of nature will apply. There is a likelihood that much of science will be capable of explanation in mathematical terms. These are all aspects of science that tend to distinguish it from other forms of thought.

Scientists tend to work within a scientific community. The opinions of the peer group are of paramount importance. A theory is unlikely to survive if not accepted by the scientific community as a whole. There is nevertheless competition between scientists. There was a race to find the composition of the double helix of DNA, which led to an understanding of the mechanism of genetics. Many scientists now work in teams, partly because of the expense of equipment and the funding of particular projects. Of course, the role of the individual genius has been and always will be of much importance.

Newton's understanding of the theory of gravity, which has underpinned all physical science at a cosmic level, was reached in a totally individual way. But it followed the pattern of being able to explain a whole range of physical processes, of being susceptible to mathematical explanation, and of being able to fit – indeed underwrite – the laws of nature. (Newton's extraordinary scientific insights he found quite compatible with religious thought.) When Einstein modified Newton's ideas with the theory of relativity, his theory stemmed from individual insight into new experimental results, yet fitted the mathematical picture of the universe. Creativity plays its part in science, but, unlike artistic activity, it is not self-sufficient and the flash of insight will be of no use unless it fits into the scientific world-pattern. Neither Newton nor Einstein's theories would have stood the test of time if the universe could not be demonstrated to have an ordered, mathematical, logical nature.

Another important aspect of science is the ability of its theories to predict: the theories of aerodynamics would not be accepted if aeroplanes did not leave the ground. Yet, there is always the possibility of a new theory based on observation and experiment, a re-ordering of our understanding, a rethink of what we know. This is what makes science exciting: the opponents of science, to whom we shall return, do not seem to understand this, when they criticise the dull, mechanical, materialistic picture of the world which they wrongly assume scientists have.

Two key scientific theories for humanists are the theory of evolution of the species by natural selection and the theory of cosmic origins in a 'big bang'. They do not preclude a belief in a god – who might have set in place the process of evolution and left it to work itself out according to certain principles or who might have set off the big bang, a divine firework, with the object of watching the universe expand into a myriad of cosmic phenomena. Yet, these two theories prompt humanists to deny a deistic explanation of universal origins.

The theory of evolution is now almost completely accepted – apart from the kick-back of a number of Creationists, particularly in the US. There is querying and debating of the mechanism of evolution and continuing data adds to the picture which Darwin originally put forward. Darwin's *On the Origin of Species by Natural Selection* (1859) created a tremendous stir in the scientific world and shook the intellectual currents of the nineteenth century. The Biblical assumption that human beings and all the other species had been created separate and complete from the beginning by a creator was shattered. Scientists such as Thomas Huxley expounded the theory and defended science in the face of religious opposition. It was thought shocking that humans were close relatives of the apes. The discovery from geological observation of the length of time that the earth and the species had taken to evolve disturbed those who took biblical time spans literally. There seemed a real conflict between religion and science – seen, for instance, in the notable book *A History of the Warfare of Science with Theology in Christendom* (Draper, 1876).

Today the majority of scientists hold non-religious beliefs and many who hold religious beliefs do not hold orthodox positions. Although many theologians came to reconcile themselves to the idea that God's purposes were seen in the evolutionary process, it might be queried as to why a process so 'red in tooth and claw', in which nature consisted of so much destruction, was chosen by the Almighty.

The phrase 'survival of the fittest', used to describe the way in which biological adaptation to the environment led to survival, has been frequently misused to justify and promote the competitiveness of human beings and human groups. Social Darwinism that aims to defend the desirability of competing as a means of progress is entirely erroneous. The idea of evolution has been frequently misunderstood to suggest that nature has 'evolved' towards the summit of its achievement – human beings. But at one point it seemed as if the progress of evolution was towards the hegemony of dinosaurs! At a future point human beings may be seen to have been a byway on the history of evolution. Of course, other factors than adaptation have affected biological processes: the dinosaurs probably disappeared as a result of an asteroid hitting the earth and the continuity of human life may depend on the extent to which human beings destroy their environment by their own activities.

The detailed mechanism of evolution was not completely understood by Darwin. With the development of an understanding of genetics and then DNA, the theory of evolution reached new levels of explanation. The gene is the essential reproductive method of living things. It adds to Darwin's theories an explanation of the method of adaptation. The reproduction of characteristics via the gene is subject to occasional error and it is from these mutations that new strains are developed and a minute number of them may prove more adaptive. DNA, the chemical component of the gene, has led to an understanding of the process of human reproduction – and indeed all organic replication. One of the most eloquent scientists explaining evolution today is Richard Dawkins – now the Charles Simonyi Professor of Public Understanding of Science at Oxford University. He has written of the 'selfish gene' as a way of describing the process whereby the gene works for its own continuity, rather than the continuity of the species.

Dawkins states: 'Not only does the Darwinian theory command superabundant power to explain. Its economy in doing so has a sinewy elegance, a poetic beauty that outclasses even the most haunting of the world's origin myths.' There are still grounds for argument about aspects of the evolutionary process. One disputed point is how far the process was gradual or how far it moved with sudden bursts – the 'punctuated equilibrium' theory. Some critics say that evolution is only a theory and cannot be proven because it can't be tested by experiment. Well, yes, the whole of science consists of a gamut of theories – but theories that work and theories that remain consistent with the evidence before us. It is possible to see species adaptation in the world. African elephants have been shot for their tusks throughout the twentieth century. Elephants with shorter tusks or no tusks are developing as an adaptation – since large tusked animals are less likely to survive. There may be a counter consequence whereby tuskless elephants have less ability to fight or forage. Numerous examples could be given of evolution observed in process.

The Creationists who reject the theory of evolution in favour of biblical description are largely evangelical Christians. They are not numerically significant among scientists, but they have made quite a noise, especially within the US. The extent to which they are taken seriously – largely by non-scientists

– suggests a wide lack of understanding of science. There has been a drive in America to teach 'Creation science' in schools as a balance to Darwinian evolution. This is really an expression of fear of secular humanism which some have tried to have banned from schools as a 'religion'. It is necessary patiently to refute the Creationists' ideas, carefully showing that their contentions are not consistent with the scientific approach. But this task may be difficult with those who do not accept the premises of science.

Evolution theory explains the development of species, but it does not explain the origin of life. At what point matter – probably in the depths of the sea – started replicating itself, it is not known. Very early forms of bacterial life have been found. Also the kind of chemical-electrical environment which might be conducive to molecular replication is increasingly being understood.

Humanists do not think that we have reached a point where we can explain everything – far from it.

Another area, where much research is being done, but there are as yet no conclusive theories, is the nature of consciousness: although our understanding of the brain is increasing a great deal, it is not yet clear at what point the ability to be self-conscious has arisen and where that ability is located.

Another searching question to which we do not have the full answer is where human beings developed – geographically and historically. The origin of the 'human family' probably goes back 7 million years, the origin of the enlarged brain 2.5 million years and the origin of *homo sapiens* perhaps 35,000 years at which point language and self-consciousness and art and technology arose. There is still much discussion as to whether *homo sapiens* arose in one geographic spot, probably Africa, or there was a multi-regional origin. The important fact here is that there is no doubt that fossil and archaeological evidence are increasingly giving us evidence of the development of the human species.

As important as human origins is the nature of matter, which links to cosmological origins. Study of the nature of the atom and then of particle physics led to an increased understanding of the nature of the universe. Heisenberg used the phrase 'the uncertainty principle' to describe the fact that it is not possible to measure the position and velocity of a particle at the same time – the more exact your measurement of the one the less certain your measurement of the other. The phrase 'uncertainty principle' – the literal translation of the German word *Ungenauigkeit* is *inexactness* – does not lead to the view that we are living in an entirely uncertain universe. The misleading implication – often taken up by non-scientists – that the whole basis of science is uncertain, traduces Heisenberg's theory, while suggesting what a hunger there is to debunk science.

There are now largely agreed theories as to the origin of the universe. It is thought that the universe started with a Big Bang 10 to 15 billion years ago and is constantly expanding. Astronomical observations have re-inforced the evidence of this outward motion. There is a theory that gravity may cause it eventually to implode in a big Crunch. An expanding and imploding universe might have no beginning and end. The role of a deity is unnecessary in either case – although theists can be happy with the Big Bang theory as an initial act of theistic creation. These theories depend upon the nature of matter in the universe. The search for an understanding of the nature of matter and the laws of nature by which it is governed is sometimes described as TOE – the Theory Of Everything. My guess is that for many centuries we will only arrive at the TOAE – the Theory of Almost Everything.

The last paragraph of Stephen Hawking's famous *A Brief History of Time* (1988) refers to the possibility of discovering a complete theory of what the universe is and why it is here.

> However, if we do discover a complete theory, it should in time be understandable in broad principle by everyone, not just a few scientists. Then we shall all, philosophers, scientists, and just ordinary people, be able to take part in the discussion of the question of why it is that we and the universe exist. If we find the answer to that, it would be the ultimate triumph of human reason – for then we would know the mind of God.

Putting aside the idea that ordinary people may one day understand the most complex of scientific concepts, this is a question-begging paragraph. Does that mean that knowledge of the 'mind of the universe' is dependent on further scientific understanding, or is knowing the mind of God merely a metaphorical statement, the mind of God being no more nor less than the totality of the universe?

In recent decades there has been a current of anti-science and pseudo science. Anti-science stems partly from a lack of understanding of science, but there are other reasons. People sometimes blame the use of scientific discoveries on the process of science itself. Once something has been discovered, it is difficult to prevent knowledge spreading and technological developments occurring. A classic instance in the twentieth century was the discovery of the atomic bomb – which became possible following developments in particle physics. Scientists, such as Einstein and Niels Bohr deeply regretted the use of some of their discoveries in this way. But it is the military and political people who pushed for the development and use of the bomb. The pollution of the earth and damage to the ecosphere (see chapter 10) are also sometimes thought to result from scientific developments. If there had been no motor car, if there had been no pesticides, if there had been no CHCs …. It is not possible to halt the development of scientific research for fear of the possible damage that the use of scientific discoveries may result in. The division between scientific research and applied science may not be completely clear cut. Humanists, however, would support moves to work for the responsible use of scientific research.

Another source of anti-science currents is the specialisation which means that almost no one understands the totality of scientific research; the biologist researching into the genome may not understand the particle physicist, very few people understand the mathematics of the evidence for the expanding universe.

Some critics of science are inclined to ask if science has been for the greater good or the greater harm. You can argue whether the development of penicillin outweighs the development of nerve gas, what are the mixed progress from the television and the computer. But you cannot stop science. The motives underlying scientific careers and research are mixed – like motives for most human behaviour. Sheer curiosity may impel some scientific researchers, but the profit underlying the discovery of a new pharmaceutical development, or the benefits (or not) to agriculture of genetically modified plants, or the prestige attached to scientific awards, or the altruism of researching a vaccine against AIDS may also motivate scientists in their work.

Pseudo-science is different from anti-science in that it proposes scientific theories not based within the normal processes of science. Homeopathy for instance, although there are many who will offer anecdotal evidence, has not as yet been explained in scientific terms – there is no theory behind it and it does not fit in with other scientific theories. How much time should be spent researching a theory which seems to have no basis? That may have been the case with much scientific research work at some times. Astrology is another pseudo-science – though it seems surprising that its supporters even want to call it a science. Many people would like to prove that personality and future life depend upon the stars – but there is no evidence, nor is it possible to see what could be the scientific evidence of such an approach.

Of course, scientists recognise that all has not yet been discovered, indeed they are eager to take part in the continuing discoveries. They also recognise the limitations of science. Science won't necessarily make us happy, or enhance our personal relationships, or help us come to terms with death. Science is not rigid or triumphant, it is continually changing and humble before the extraordinariness of the world and the universe. Science is rather like Hume's description of the truth: 'truth being always in use but always under reconstruction.'

One of the reasons for anti-science and pseudo-science is that human beings find it hard to accept the idea of a random universe and a universe without purpose. We are so intent on creating purposes for our own lives and for the lives of our societies, that we baulk at the idea of a purposeless universe. Kant in his *Principle of Natural Purposefulness* said that we cannot prove that Nature is purposefully organised, but must co-ordinate data as though it were. To accept that the universe may not care for human beings may seem bleak. The words of the poet A. E. Housman express it well:

> For Nature, heartless, witless nature
> Will neither care nor know.

Nevertheless, anyone able to surf through complex mathematics, study the natural world, or contemplate the stars above will surely possess a stimulating sense of wonder in face of the universe.

8

Humanism and the Arts

Artistic creation is an essential part of human activity. Humanists are sometimes accused of being 'dry rationalists', but of course they have emotion. In the warmth of human love for family and friends, in their marvel and wonder at the natural universe, in their passionate commitment to participating in a humane society, and in their vital appreciation of the arts they are far from dry. Iris Murdoch wrote an essay 'Against Dryness'. In her novels she gave a portrayal of the vastness of human nature and an understanding of the human condition . She was not quite a humanist – 'a religious person without a religion' her husband, John Bayley, described her. In 'Against Dryness' she wrote: 'Literature, in curing its own ills, can give us a new vocabulary of experience and a truer picture of freedom.' This could be said for all the arts and it is to be found in the flow and interplay of artistic discourse. The difficulty of grasping works of art is like the difficulty of holding water in the hand, the uncertainty within a search for truth and reality, the chameleon-like characteristic of avoiding being pinned down. The arts are in this way an important balance to excessive analysis and reasoning, to any risk of 'dryness'.

The arts are not a substitute for religion. If we wish to do without religion, we will not wish to erect a counterpart. The English Buddhist, Sangharakshita, leader of the Friends of the Western Buddhist Order, has stated that true art is a means to the communication of spiritual values. Humanists would disagree in so far as they do not want to propose art as a religion substitute. What is meant by 'spiritual' values is a large question dealt with elsewhere. But we do not believe in a god of the Beethoven late string quartets. They are what they are in their extraordinary complexity and beauty and are to be enjoyed and explored in their self-contained completeness.

Art is not an extra – the icing on the cake – but an essential part of human existence. At its best it can expand our consciousness, it can awaken us to people and experiences other than our own, it can intensify our awareness. Art is not essentially consolatory. It offers 'naught for your comfort' (Chesterton). Kafka in his notebooks expressed it very well: 'A book should be an ice-axe to break the frozen sea within us.' In his unsettling, disturbing tales, Kafka

Epicurus, Greek philosopher (341 - 270 BC)

Diderot - Leading encyclopédist (1713 - 1784)

Thomas Paine, champion of the rights of man and the age of reason (1737 - 1809)

Charles Darwin (1789 - 1882)

Charles Bradlaugh - Freethinker and parliamentarian (1833 - 1891)

Humanist University, the Netherlands

Nettie Klein (IHEU Secretary) at an international humanist event

Picture from Arthur Miller's play The Crucible

Atheist Centre (India) Jubilee Congress

Rural development children's project

certainly did that, in *The Trial* giving us a sense of universal guilt and in *The Castle* a sense of universal waiting. He explores the anguish of existence – not from social circumstances or personal unhappiness, but as a very condition of being. The greatest artists such as Shakespeare can give us much the same in, say, the agony of King Lear, while at the same time in their oeuvre give us the greatest diversity of human experience including love and joy and playfulness.

Although we can learn from it and benefit from it, art is not utilitarian; it's not just a tool for a purpose, or a slate from which we can be educated. The value that may come from reading a searing account of Auschwitz, as in Primo Levi's *If This is a Man*, is not to be calculated. The book is not functional: it just is in all its terror and glory.

The earliest human artistic creations were the cave paintings, some of which go back up to 30,000 years. The depictions of animals and humans and symbols is remarkable – making us wonder whether there has been much improvement in artistic skills in the recorded history of the human race. There is much argument about their purpose: magical control over life, religious control over the human group, establishing the cohesiveness of the tribe – all may be considered part of the original purpose. But it is very hard not to believe that, despite these purposes, an element of delight in depicting the real may have been there. Although art is not functional, we can accept that it sometimes gives cohesiveness to society (sometimes is disruptive, especially with new art).

Creating a sense of community is certainly a consequence of some art. Some arts are more social than others: the theatre is a joint activity compared to the individual process of reading a book or reading on a computer screen (reading on the page and on the screen are different kinds of experiences). The original Greek dramas were viewed by very large audiences at public festivals. Sharing an experience – comic or tragic – can strengthen the feeling of belonging to a community. The laughter or gasps together confirm that we live together, that we are social beings. Mass audiences for opera in Italy and football crowds round the world may offer similar experiences – though football may allow us to see balletic skill and give excitement in an element of conflict between parts of the audience which is not found in the theatre. Shared symbolic experiences such as the opening of parliament or a public funeral are not really artistic events, although art may be put to their service. Art is not usually at its best when created to serve the state or a public institution – think of the dismal offerings of poet laureates in their formal role over the past 300 years. Didactic art may have its place – but also its dangers. The strongest argument against didactic art – for instance some of the official works during the period of the USSR – is that it is poor and ineffective. Stalinist architecture is a byword for ugliness.

Some dramatists such as Shakespeare, Henryk Ibsen and Arthur Miller have been particularly good at creating a sense of community and the individual's place in it. Shakespeare's Histories demonstrate the interrelatedness of society from the monarch to the humble soldier. Miller's *The Crucible* depicts the whole community of Salem obsessed and possessed with a belief in witchcraft – the tragedy would not have developed but for the communal hysteria: Miller is suggesting that responsibility and loss of responsibility lie with individuals operating through the community. In Ibsen's *An Enemy of the People* the whole town turns against a doctor who points out that the baths on which their livelihood depends are polluted. Ibsen may have been influenced by the great British secularist, Charles Bradlaugh, whose stand on publishing birth control information and whose struggle to enter parliament he admired. Being part of the community while retaining one's sense of individuality and conscience are humanist principles.

E. M . Forster – an example of an artist who was an avowed humanist – created whole communities in his novels. In *Howard's End* he tried to give a complete picture of the different levels of society in England. The phrase 'only connect', with which the novel was headed, refers to the need which he saw for connections across the whole of society. Again in *Passage to India* he attempts to give a picture of society as whole – from the colonial blimps to the different groups of Indians. He expressed his longing for the coming together of different races at the end of the novel. An Englishman says to an Indian: 'Why can't we be friends now?'…. 'It's what I want. It's what you want.':

> But the horses didn't want it – they swerved apart; the earth did not want it, sending up rocks through which riders must pass single file; the temples, the tank, the jail, the palace, the birds, the carrion, the Guest House, that came into view as they issued from the gap and saw Mau beneath: they didn't want it, they said in their hundred voices, 'No, not yet,' and the sky said 'No, not there'.

Forster aches for the barriers between different groups to fall away.

Other writers have aimed to give a picture of the whole of society, Tolstoy and Zola for instance. There is also, of course, much art that is less earnest, more playful: the magical realism of some modern novels, abstract art, or non-referential music all attend more to our sense of delight in the play of sounds or words or ideas. The Argentinian writer Jorge Luis Borges comes into this category with his labyrinthine tales opening profound and paradoxical vistas of the complexity of human perception.

Perception of others and awareness of the community were very important to George Eliot. She shocked Victorian England by her agnosticism and her

unmarried partnership with G. E. Lewes. In her first full length novel, *Adam Bede* she writes:

> So I am content to tell my simple story, without trying to make things seem better than they were; dreading nothing, indeed, but falsity, which, in spite of one's best efforts, there is no reason to dread. Falsehood is so easy, truth so difficult. The pencil is conscious of a delightful facility in drawing a griffin – the longer the claws, and the larger the wings, the better; but that marvellous facility which we mistake for genius is apt to forsake us when we want to draw a real unexaggerated lion. Examine your words well, and you will find that even when you have no motive to be false, it is a very hard thing to say the exact truth, even about your own immediate feelings – much harder than to say something fine about them which is not the truth.

Seeking the truth, telling the truth are aims of most artists. Recent post-modern thinkers tell us that there is no such thing as truth and all art is a discourse relative to its own existence. But I think artists and critics will always want truth as a touchstone of what they are trying to do.

In reading about other people or viewing portraits we gain by an imaginative sympathy a glimpse of what it is not to be ourselves. This is difficult for human beings bound within their own selfhood. The arts can enlarge and enrich our knowledge of the diversity of humanity, to cross boundaries of nation, of race, of time.

Through art we enlarge our own boundaries. At its highest this could contribute to a global ethic or a sense of 'universal sympathy'. I am not suggesting this should necessarily be its aim, but may be its effect. Thomas Mann, one of the greatest novelists of the twentieth century, in a late and uncharacteristically humorous novel, *The Confessions of Felix Krull, Confidence Man* (1954) described a naturalist talking to the confidence trickster about the progress of humanity from its natural raw material to self-conscious creatures:

> Being was not Well-Being; it was joy and labour, and all Being in space-time, all matter, partook if only in deepest sleep in this joy and labour, this perception that disposed Man, possessor of the most awakened consciousness, to universal sympathy.

This universal sympathy, coming from empathy with all creation can be an important part of art. It is not that we sympathise with everyone, or that we are taught a lesson about the global ethic, but that the consciousness of the separateness of other people and of the natural world enhances our consciousness and frees us from our obsession with our selves.

Although there has been much emphasis here upon literature, the visual and aural arts are equally important. There are musicians with a specific humanist outlook (Delius for instance) but it is not in the avowed religious or non-religious views that humanist will enjoy music. A number of agnostic or at least highly unorthodox composers have written religious works: Verdi's *Requiem* or Benjamin Britten's *War Requiem*, Janacek's *Glagolitic Mass*. Michael Tippett, one of the greatest twentieth century English composers, although retaining some mystical ideas, was close to humanism in many of his ideas: his early oratorio *The Child of our Time*, expressed profound concern for a pre-war Jewish pogrom; his late oratorio, *The Mask of Time* looked deeply at the nature of the human condition. Humanists can appreciate the profound beauty and emotion of Bach's St Matthew Passion and St John Passion: to humanists the story will have a mythical rather than a theological framework, but it is not the less moving.

The activity of playing or singing is itself often a communal one – the interplay with other voices, human or musical, is an integral part of the artistic experience. The experience of playing in a school orchestra or singing in a school choir can be enormously rewarding: and it brings self-discipline, co-operation, harnessing of the emotions, acting with precision, preparing carefully for a goal: what could be more educational – and yet schools have at the time of writing been forced to cut down musical activities because of financial constraints.

There is no simple equation pitting the humanism of renaissance art against the religious iconography of medieval art. It is quite possible for humanists to appreciate religious art as it is possible for religious people to appreciate secular art. Nevertheless, there is a direct movement into the realm of the human with renaissance art. The emphasis on the human face, in say Leonardo's Mona Lisa or the human body in the Davids of Donatello and Michaelangelo, produced a new worldly aspect to painting and sculpture. The Dutch domestic scenes of the seventeenth century give a reality of the kind which George Eliot referred to:

> It is for this rare, precious quality of truthfulness that I delight in many Dutch paintings, which lofty-minded people despise. I find a source of delicious sympathy in these faithful pictures of a monotonous homely existence, which has been the fate of so many more among my fellow-mortals than a life of pomp or of absolute indigence, of tragic suffering or of world-stirring actions. I turn, without shrinking, from cloud-borne angels, from prophets, sybils, and heroic warriors, to an old woman bending over her flower-pot, or eating her solitary dinner, while the noonday light, softened perhaps by a screen of leaves, falls on her mob-cap, and just touches the rim of her spinning-wheel, and her stone jug, and all those cheap common things which are the precious necessities

of life to her; – or I turn to that village wedding, kept between four brown walls, where an awkward bridegroom opens the dance with a high-shouldered, broad-faced bride, while elderly and middle-aged friends look on, with very irregular noses and lips, and probably with quart pots in their hands, but with an expression of unmistakeable contentment and goodwill.

Not all humanists will wish to forsake grandeur, but it is the sheer reality, which we might find in a Rembrandt portrait, that appeals and makes us look at the world afresh. In the twentieth century it might be thought that the development of abstract art was a move aware from the human, but Picasso never lost sight of this dimension. Picasso's painting Guernica, a picture relating to the Spanish Civil War, is impelled by a sense of social consciousness. In the most abstract of Henry Moore's sculptures, we can sense the human within the stone. Even where the artist is religious or semi-religious it is the appeal to our sense of shape and colour, as well as to the human, which enlarges our consciousness.

Art is neither optimistic nor pessimistic. It must take on the bleak aspect of human existence, but it can, if not provide meaning, at least enable us to work out our own sense of the meaning of life. Artists have felt deeply the starkness of human life. Jonathan Swift, author of the great satire *Gulliver's Travels*, wrote his own epitaph which is to be found in Dublin Cathedral where he is buried: 'Here is laid the body of Jonathan Swift, Doctor of Divinity, Dean of this Cathedral Church where savage indignation can no longer tear his heart. Go traveller, and imitate if you can one who strove with all his might to champion liberty.' The savage indignation – seen in Gulliver's visit to the land of the Yahoos – and the defence of liberty are both important themes in the humanist understanding of art.

Samuel Beckett, as novelist and playwright, took on the bleakest possible aspect of the world. All his characters are in extremity. In *Malone Dies*, the protagonist lies in bed through the novel, apparently dying – but he keeps himself going by telling stories to himself with no audience. For Beckett's characters the world seems absurd and meaningless, but yet in the stoic potential for survival there is a redeeming glimpse of the hope necessary to keep going.

Waiting for Godot, which was one of the most admired plays of the second half of the twentieth century, contains two clown/tramps waiting for the unexplained Godot who never arrives. One of the characters says – 'They give birth astride of a grave, the light gleams an instant, then it's night once more' and this sentiment pervades the play. Yet somewhere between the birth and the death there are possibilities of survival and meaning, although this can hardly be seen as optimism. Humanism has to take on the profound pessimism of

writers such as Beckett who wrote of himself: 'I could not have gone through the awful wretched mess of life without having left a stain upon the silence.' This is a potent metaphor for artistic activity, its desperation and its necessity.

Another writer who took on the bleakness of life was the novelist Virginia Woolf. She suffered from depression and eventually committed suicide. Yet her novels contain a breadth and sensitivity which is anything but depressing. In *Mrs Dalloway*, one character sitting in the park observes: 'For the truth is that human beings have neither kindness nor faith, nor charity beyond what serves to increase the pleasure of the moment. They hunt in packs. Their packs scour the desert and vanish screaming into the wilderness. They desert the fallen. They are plastered over with grimaces.' Although it is not possible to interpret one passage of a novel as representing the author's views, in all her works there is a sense of 'the skull beneath the skin', of what lies under the veneer of civilization. Humanists, whose view of human beings is often considered too rosy, need the darker side as reflected in writers like Beckett and Virginia Woolf.

Satire – developing from Swift's 'savage indignation' – is a powerful tool for social comment. Orwell's *Nineteen Eighty-Four* and *Animal Farm* are examples of the use of satire and a dystopia to attack totalitarianism. Writers such as Solzhenitsyn in novels such as *One Day in the Life of Ivan Denisovich* graphically depict the sufferings of people from the dictatorship of Stalin. Although art's function is not essentially social comment, many writers feel a sense of responsibility. In the case of Brecht, his determination that his plays should change the world may have hindered his work, for he was at his best when he was least didactic.

Arthur Miller strongly supports the need for artists to be socially active. He wrote of his work as President of PEN (the international organisation for writers' freedom) 'Pen seemed to promise an awakening of humanist solidarity at a time when the opposing creed of untrammeled individualism and private success was beginning its most recent sweep of the American political landscape.' Humanists have felt the defence of writers – of all political complexions – to say and write as they wish, is very important. Those writers who have fallen foul of religious groups are particularly in need of such defence. Salman Rushdie, whose *Satanic Verses* (1988) caused a *fatwa* to be issued against him and a price put on his head, is a writer of great creative genius whose life has been severely constricted by the attack on him. Taslima Nasreen, the Bangladeshi novelist and poet has suffered similar attacks from fundamentalists. Rushdie has written that he regrets the offence that has been caused and that he accepts his condition 'I will strive to change it, but I inhabit it. I am trying to learn from it. Our lives teach us who we are. Art can teach us who we are as well.'

Seumus Heaney is a poet deeply concerned with humanist values (though not necessarily a humanist himself). One of his poems is particularly apt in expressing the position of the artist. *The Forge* opens with the words : 'All I know is a door into the dark'; inside the smith engages in his practical, earthy creation; but ultimately all artists – and all of us – know no more than the door in the dark. In the acceptance speech which Heaney gave when he accepted the Nobel Prize for literature, he concluded:

> The form of the poem, in other words, is crucial to poetry's power to do the thing which always is and always will be to poetry's credit: the power to persuade that vulnerable part of our consciousness of its rightness in spite of the evidence of wrongness all around it, the power to remind us that we are hunters and gatherers of values, that our very solitudes and distresses are creditable, in so far as they, too, are an earnest of our veritable human being.

All art attends to our vulnerability and loneliness, and seeks human values for this condition while asserting our humanness as social and individual beings.

9

Humanism and the Environment

Environmental issues may be more important than any of the other subjects covered in this book. It is imperative that humanists take account of the colossal environmental problems facing life on earth. There are ethical issues – and survival issues even – in potential climate change, species decline, stewardship for future generations, pollution, population growth and genetic modification.

The classic critique of humanism in this field came from David Erhenfeld in *The Arrogance of Humanism* (1981). He states that although humanism 'has its nobler parts' – 'we have been too gentle and uncritical of it in the past, and it has grown ugly and dangerous. Humanism itself, like the rest of our existence, must now be protected against its own excesses. Fortunately there are humane alternatives to the arrogance of humanism'. The philosopher Jürgen Habermas in *Towards a Rational Society* queried the dominance of technocratic rationality. The attitude of communists to the environment exemplified this attitude to nature. It was stated in relation to the Programme of the Soviet Communist Party, approved in 1961 at its Second Party Conference: 'Communism elevates man to a tremendous level of supremacy over nature and makes possible a greater and fuller use of its inherent forms'.

There are others who criticise humanism for its relationship to the 'enlightenment project', for its belief in the human ability to create progress, for its overemphasis on the human, for its blind belief in science. Humanists have to answer some of these criticisms seriously. At the same time there is in the Green movement an element of mysticism and sentimentality that humanists can do without.

Humanists have to consider the grounds for stewardship of the planet for future generations, for a balance between life for humans and for other species, for creating the conditions for sustainability, for the eliciting of human values in the face of potential nihilism.

Does it matter if human life dies out on earth – just as the life of dinosaurs did?

It is probable that even with the destruction of most species – including the human one – micro-organisms which can survive under extreme heat or water pressure would provide the starting point for the redevelopment, probably eventually differently, of diversity of species on earth again. Does it matter if all human life disappears on the planet? We are not there to regret our own death, likewise we would not be there to regret the end of the human species. In any case, there is a probability that there is life elsewhere in the universe, which may be sufficient to satisfy our instinct that life should continue somewhere.

Most humanists would argue for the need to attempt to preserve life on this planet. This may stem from the evolutionary instinct for survival. It is partly a desire to see the generations that follow us prosper. The argument for intergenerational responsibility is strong. If there is ultimately no meaning in the universe, there is nevertheless the meaning that we wish to give our lives and the lives of our successors. Humanists have been accused of being 'speciesist', that is emphasising the human at the expense of the non-human, but most humanists would recognise a sense of responsibility for ourselves and for future generations, and for other species. Humanists believe deeply in values (see chapter on ethics) which could extend beyond the pre-eminent position of human beings. Humanist morality is largely based on reciprocity, but what reciprocity can there be between humans today and humans tomorrow. Our behaviour to others can be affected by our ability to empathise with and understand them. Such empathy can be extended to other than human species such as primates or to future living creatures. Many, including humanists, can commit themselves beyond the human and the contemporary. If so, perhaps they would put more force behind attempts to do something about the situation, for it is clear that humanity as a whole finds it extremely difficult to put the safety of future humans before their own personal comfort.

The environment issue which stands before all others is that of climate change. Of course, growth of population and depletion of resources also present dire threats. But personally, I think it is climate change about which we run the risk of taking action too late to avoid enormous devastation.   Many scientists consider the evidence of the beginning of climate change to be conclusive. They base their theories on changes in existing climate patterns, on computer models of what could happen as a result of the increase in greenhouse gases, especially carbon dioxide from the burning of fossil fuels. Continuing planetary warming is predicted. 'The average temperature of the world is now 0.8 per cent C higher than it was in 1900. The Intergovernmental Panel on Climate Change expects the temperature to rise by a further 3 per cent C by 2100.' (*New Scientist*, 1 July 2000). Consequences are thought likely to be melting of the polar ice caps, rise in sea level (drowning low lying regions, such as Bangla Desh), alteration in movement of sea currents and wind patterns with unpredictable results on weather, drought in Africa and even the

Mediterranean in places such as southern Italy. New and dangerous patterns of disease are likely to develop. Water and food shortages will become more severe.

This model needs to be accepted with caution. There might be other reasons for climate change than the greenhouse effect. Some point to the effect of changes in the state of the sun on weather. It is equally important to remember that during the 3.5 to 4 billion years that the earth has existed there have been enormous climate changes. The movement of continents, the shift in ocean currents, and the cycles of glaciation have all brought great climate change through the millennia. Nevertheless scientists increasingly consider that there is evidence for an irreversible shift in the climate on earth. If we want to do something about it, there is no use waiting until it has happened.

Most people feel fatalistic about such enormous changes, finding it difficult to grasp what might happen and what we might do. Governments have met to search for a solution and an agreement to do something about it. A reduction in the burning of fossil fuels is a key proposal. Agreements for reduction have been made, but are only a starting point and seem unlikely to be adhered to. The industrial countries, which burn huge quantities of oil in cars would find it extremely difficult to change their transport patterns. The US in particular is wedded to a gas-guzzling way of life in which people's right to drive large cars for virtually all travel is seen as an inalienable right; overheated dwellings are another factor. The rejection of the Kyoto Treaty by President G. W. Bush confirms this anti-social attitude. The need to live a less energy spending life-style is likely to be very difficult to follow. The West uses a much higher proportion of energy than the rest of the world in ratio to the size of its population. Deforestation is another factor, and the profit-motive of land clearance is much stronger than the desire to create a sustainable future.

Politicians bow to the wishes of those living today rather than tomorrow – their time-scale is the next election, rather than the next generation. Green parties have attained minority positions in power, without the potential for changing much other than small environmental points, such as improved cycling tracks or increased tree planting in parks. Humanists have not as a whole organised campaigns on green issues, though individuals have been very active. Perhaps humanists, cognizant of the possible threats to the environment, should include environmental issues much more prominently in their programmes and activity. Let's be clear we need international agreements, not just bottle recycling banks (valuable as recycling may be). The international conferences dealing with environment and climate in Rio de Janeiro and Kyoto, for instance, have brought overwhelming scientific evidence of impending trouble, attempts at agreement between governments which have not been kept, and a weird combination of urgency and evasion.

The concept of 'sustainability' is extremely important: modifying the behaviour of human beings on the planet to maintain bio-diversity, endurable climate for humans, sufficient food and energy for survival, an environment without threatening toxicity, a level of population increase (or decrease) that is commensurate with resources available. In order to be fully human, we will need to be fully in balance with the earth's nature – not in any mystical sense, but in the hard-headed sense of existence that takes into account more than its own being. The influential environmental writer, Theodore Roszak, has written 'By becoming so aggressively and masterfully "human", we lose our essential humanity'. Humanists , with their emphasis on the human, would not wish to lose their essential humanity.

Sheer numbers may threaten sustainability. The population of about 6 billion at the beginning of the third millenium is expected to grow to 8.25 billion by 2015 and possibly to stabilise at around 10 billion by 2050.The growth will not be distributed evenly around the world: AIDS may significantly reduce population size in some regions. In Western countries, a lower birth rate may cause population to decline, with an ageing population creating economic problems. In continents such as Asia the population is expanding greatly. Population control is seen as essential. (Those religious groups who oppose contraception – and the use of condoms to prevent the spread of HIV – are seriously anti-humanitarian.) The quality of life, for instance in Mumbai (Bombay) has deteriorated considerably in the last 30 years because of population pressures. China has made successful attempts to control the rise of population, with authoritarian rules. The conflict between authoritarian approaches and individual liberty can be seen in this and other environmental issues. Could we take away people's right to run large cars? Humanists have tended to emphasise individual liberty, but would they accept some authoritarian rules to bring about long term improvement of the environment?

Humanists have been in the forefront of moves to stabilise population growth. Annie Besant, the nineteenth-century secularist, supported the publication of a book giving details of means of birth control and was, together with Charles Bradlaugh, tried for publishing it, narrowly escaping prison. A leading radical humanist in India, Mrs Parikh, founded an organisation for bringing birth control information to women in the slums of Mumbai. The evidence is clear that education of women especially with knowledge of infant welfare which ensures the growth of the child into adulthood is an important factor in population control. One of the problems of population growth is that it increases the inequity between developed and undeveloped countries. Perhaps the importance of population limitation has been overemphasised – it is a soluble problem, and could be solved in the next 50 years. Indeed, the situation has improved considerably in China, Indonesia and the State of Kerala in India. Nevertheless pressure from population growth is a huge problem in many parts of the world. The ability to feed an increased population is probably there – with redistribution and possibly GM modified crops. But the quality of life might be grim and the pressure of economic migration to wealthier parts of the world enormous.

While we consider the rights of humans to have large families, people are beginning to consider the rights of non-human animals. Do apes have rights? They are remarkably close to humans in DNA constitution and in evolutionary development. They seem to have linguistic ability, self-consciousness, and an instinct for group and individual relationships. The utilitarian philosopher, Jeremy Bentham (1748 – 1832), with remarkable prescience considered that his felicific calculus should apply to all sentient beings: the 'greatest number' for whom the 'greatest happiness' should be available, included the animal kingdom. The philosopher, Peter Singer, has argued all sentient animals are morally equal. But where does sentience begin? The problem is where to draw the dividing line – should we be considering the greatest happiness of all forms of life – the malaria-infected mosquito, the HIV virus?

Those who defend animal rights particularly criticise animal experiments: here we have to weigh the right of the animal – mouse or cat say – against the benefit to the human race. Obviously, there should be minimising of suffering, but should we, for instance, forego the chance of a vaccine for AIDS, the cause of such enormous and increasing death and suffering across the world, rather than test on animals? The use of cell culture may reduce, although it is unlikely to eliminate, the need for animal experiments. The case of animal experiments is a real test of how human-centred your philosophy is. (Vegetarianism, which has increased so much in Britain in the last twenty years, is of a piece with such thought.) Some argue that animals have rights in so far as they have value to us, others that animals have intrinsic rights – that the animal is not there to benefit us or even the ecosphere, but has its own rights. Those who consider all living creatures have an important existence of their own would consider that it enriches the world and ourselves to see the human as only a part of the whole.

The ability to think of the earth as a whole rather than our individual place in it is important to humanists. The damage of pollution and exploitation may not threaten in the same way as climate change, but there is clear damage to the environment and our existence within it. One of the first significant writers on the environment, was Rachel Carson, whose *Silent Spring* first drew attention to the effect of indiscriminate use of insecticides and demonstrated how toxic chemicals could enter the chain of existence. She wrote: 'The "control of nature" is a phrase conceived in arrogance, born of the neanderthal age of biology and philosophy, when it was supposed nature exists for the convenience of man.' It is possible that pesticides in the food chain and in plastics may be causing cancer and other illness. Insects rapidly become resistant to pesticides, which are therefore no long-term solution.

The dangers of nuclear waste, of oil spillages and so on to the environment have been much discussed. There is a question of balance of risk to be considered: is the value of nuclear power greater than the risk of pollution or accident? Is the need for petrol more important than the danger of oil spills? There may be need for a calculus of risk. The concept of risk is widely misunderstood as is instanced by people's greater fear of travelling in an aeroplane than of driving a car.

The issue of genetically modified crops has become very controversial. There is great fear that modified crops will contaminate surrounding wild life, that genetic changes might affect the human gut. People talk about Frankenstein food and the ethics of creating new species. Scientific research is a better way to cope with these changes than fear. Nevertheless the predicted benefits of genetic modification to increase yields to feed a growing world population, reduction of the need for pesticides, reduced soil erosion because of less turning of the soil may be exaggerated. Crops resistant to disease and insects may spread to create resistant weeds. Pests may prove to have the same power of resistance to genetic modifications as to insecticides. There may be other ways of feeding the poor, such as a fairer distribution of food. Also the so-called 'terminator' technology which creates infertile seeds, suggests that commercial companies are more interested in profit than in improving the feeding system. Social networks for the distribution and sale of food are as important as the production of the food. Low tech solutions create better solutions than high tech ones which aim to bring big profits to western companies.

There are much more drastic possibilities of gene modification within animal species – pigs creating medical products, microbes that eat toxic waste, the ideas have only just begun. As with human genetic modification an ethical code of practice should be developed which allows for scientific research but maintains the 'precautionary principle'.

Humanists will be very concerned with the ethics of genetic modification. The principle of reciprocity, the need to prevent dangers for the community as a whole, the need to base principles and practice on evidence, are all factors to consider. The humanist concern with values leads us to accept that we need to consider more than the merely human: the future of the planet and the respect for other species need to be there. Perhaps there is a need to develop the Universal Declaration of Human Rights to cover the responsibilities towards future generations and the integrity of the earth. Perhaps we shall eventually have to deal with questions of reciprocity with other parts of the universe.

Some are suspicious of the value of science (see chapter 8). The environmental campaigner, Jonathon Porritt, has called for 'science with soul'. Scientists should take more trouble to explain their research to the public: ignorance is not a blessing. Although scientific research at any one moment or place is bound to be affected by the society and historic moment within which it is found, scientific experiments and results are universal in their understanding and application.

Science is not value free, say some critics. Of course, there are scientists employed by chemical companies or government defence departments, whose research is influenced by their employer. But eventually the results and theories of science are free for all to use and develop. Scientists will have personal values that underpin their work, but it is not because of these values that they find a particular scientific result. There is a need for scientists to work at an understanding of the creation of sustainability on the earth. There is a call for science to be more 'holistic' and not reduce everything to its component parts (reductionism): but nothing could be more holistic than the theories of Darwin or Einstein.

The Gaia theory, first proposed by James Lovelock, began as a scientific theory but developed in some quarters into a mystical ideal. Gaia is defined as 'a complex entity involving the Earth's biosphere, atmosphere, oceans, and soil; the totality consisting of a feedback or cybernetic system which seeks an optimal physical and chemical environment for life on this planet.' We may not accept that the system is inherently self-conscious, but we have to accept that it has operated with an overall balance that has increasingly and seriously been upset over the last few decades. Lovelock saw this as a hypothesis and also suggested that the balance between the needs of humans and the planet needs to change. Interpreters of the Gaia hypothesis have adopted views that suggest that there is a quasi-religious nature to the balance of earth. Certainly, one of the key concepts of modern eco-theory is the interconnectedness of everything on earth.

Theorists and activists in ecological thought can be seen as anthropocentric or ecocentric 'greens' – those who still give the human a central place and those who put the ecosphere before any human considerations. The division is seen in the attitude to population and to land use: the ecocentric Greens consider that population should ultimately be reduced on earth and also that land should be set aside to return to wild. Ecologists discuss deeply the need to reconcile democracy with the authoritarian rule that might be needed to bring about change which people are reluctant to follow. So-called 'deep ecology' argues for 'biospherical egalitarianism' – the recognition that all organisms in a biosphere, or ecological zone, have an equal right to live and thrive.

Humanists can extend their belief that we have an integral part in our human community to a feeling that we can relate to the earth as a whole. It is a gut human feeling that humans and other life on earth should survive, although on the scale of the universe it may not be significant. We are in the process of extending our sympathies from our local community, to our nation, to the earth as a whole.

We may be pessimistic about human survival, but some of the changes necessary to bring it about might be liberating. The momentum for material progress, the desire to dominate, the desire of governments to please too easily, masculine assertiveness might all be changed with benefit. Christopher Stone in defending the rights of non-human beings stated that we need 'a clear change of consciousness from the point of making us far better humans'. The environment writer based at the Atheist Centre (Vijayawada, India), Vikas Gora, has suggested that the protection of the environment is the result of a new value system: 'Conservation is a conscious act and it may involve changing priorities, forgoing immediate advantages and striving for a better future which involves not only individual benefit, but also of society at large.'

Theodore Roszak suggests that 'the environmental anguish of Earth has entered our lives as a radical transformation of identity'. Nehru, writing before major environmental concerns had widely developed, posited that 'Man no longer sees nature as something apart and distinct from himself. Human destiny appears to become a part of nature's rhythmic energy.' (*The Discovery of India*, 1960) Humanism can be strengthened by embracing the extra-human world and humanists may be enlarged by understanding their place within the non-human.

10 Organised Humanism

Humanism can survive as a philosophy of life in a wide variety of societies and with individual thinkers promoting its ideas without any organized humanist movement. However, there have arisen in Britain (and there are comparable organisations in other countries) a number of humanist organizations, which in various ways attempt to promote humanist ideas, humanist values, and humanist mutual support.

The national humanist organizations in Britain are the National Secular Society, the South Place Ethical Society, the Rationalist Press Association, the British Humanist Association and the Gay and Lesbian Humanist Association. There is also a network of humanist local groups across the country. Scotland and Northern Ireland have successful regional organizations and publications. Most of these organizations are member organizations of the International Humanist and Ethical Union.

People often ask why there are several humanist organizations rather than one within which all humanists can put their energies and resources. It might indeed be a good idea to link up the organizations if starting afresh. But the existing organizations have different historical origins and distinct emphases. There is a strand originating from utopian co-operative groups and working class radicalism and there is a strand with roots in the non-conformist chapel and eventually ethical church: from these two strands come secularism and ethicism. There can in particular be a difference of approach between those who wish to clear the ground by attacking religion and those who wish to lay stress on ethical behaviour and ethical ideals.

The National Secular Society

The National Secular Society was founded in 1866 by Charles Bradlaugh. There already existed a number of isolated secular groups based around the remnants of co-operative groups founded by the early socialist and founder of the Co-operative movement, Robert Owen. G. J. Holyoake, who had been imprisoned for blasphemy, wanted to organise groups to oppose 'the vast organized error of religion'. In 1851 he addressed a group of 300 in the London Hall of Science – and founded the Society of Reasoners. This became the Secular Society. Holyoake was attracted to the positive connotations of the word 'secularism' liking to quote the French positivist Comte's words 'Nothing is destroyed until it is replaced'.

When the many local secular groups joined together as the National Secular Society, Charles Bradlaugh was their ideal leader. Born in the East End of London he quarreled with his parish clergyman at an early age and began his own careful critical study of the Bible. He developed his reasoning and oratorical powers among the open air speakers of the time. He founded the journal *The National Reformer* in 1860 and edited it (with a brief break because of ill health) until his death in 1893. It became a record of his public activities. He wanted it to be 'an avant courier on political, social and theological questions, but it should never deal with one to the entire exclusion of others'. How far to stick to specific counter-religious issues or embrace wider social issues has always been debated in the humanist movement.

Bradlaugh was the freethinker of greatest stature in the second half of the nineteenth century. Apart from his continuous work as a critic of religion in print and on the platform, two major points in his career were the *Fruits of Philosophy* trial (1877) and his struggle to enter Parliament. The *Fruits of Philosophy* was a pamphlet giving birth control advice – a very contentious subject even among freethinkers. Together with the increasingly prominent freethinker, Annie Besant, they republished the pamphlet and were tried for printing obscenity. They were found guilty and given a fine and six months imprisonment, but the verdict was quashed on appeal on a technicality. It was a key moment in the development of the right to information about sexual matters. And a number of humanists in the twentieth century have joined the struggle for information and individual rights in the sexual field.

Bradlaugh was accepted as a Parliamentary candidate for the Liberal Party and was elected for a Northampton constituency in 1880. He let it be known that he intended and thought he had the right to affirm rather than swear on the Bible when he entered the House of Commons. When he was told that no such right existed, he prepared to swear on the Bible. Opponents then claimed that his oath on the Bible would be null because he did not believe in it. During the following five year struggle for his right to enter Parliament, he was reelected by his Northampton supporters more than once. He was ejected from the House by the Sergeant of Arms and was imprisoned for a night in the Clock Tower. Finally, on the election of a Tory Parliament in 1886, at the swearing in ceremony, Bradlaugh was allowed to take the oath on the Bible. He was responsible for the Passage of Oaths Act, 1888, which gave MPs the right to affirm – a right which is rarely used by MPs today.

Bradlaugh was succeeded as President of the National Secular Society by G. W. Foote, the man who had founded *The Freethinker* in 1881. This weekly paper soon printed cartoons ridiculing the Christian faith. G. W. Foote was tried and convicted of blasphemy for some of these cartoons. He was imprisoned for a year – a punishment which even those who abhorred the cartoons thought was excessively harsh. Abolition of blasphemy law was and still is a part of the secularist programme.

During G. W. Foote's Presidency (1893 - 1915) the National Secular Society shifted from being a popular movement to being a lobby for particular causes. The secularization of society meant that much of its platform became redundant – and certainly biblical criticism and the dismantling of dogma is now done by the theologians themselves. The characteristic working class autodidacts were less common with universal education and expansion of university education. Some argued that the National Secular Society's work was done.

But there were people and a platform to keep secularism alive. Chapman Cohen was President of the NSS from 1915 to 1949 and editor of *The Freethinker* from 1915 to 1951. From a Jewish family he never identified as a Jew and shared the Association's anti-Zionist stance. He was a prolific writer and speaker concerned with the philosophy of materialism as well as the issues of the day. A vigorous President in the second half of the twentieth century has been Barbara Smoker, an ex-Catholic, who exploited the media with great effect in presenting counter-religious arguments.

Some have argued that the National Secular Society's approach is outmoded and too negative. But secularists would argue that religious influence has far from disappeared and that there continue to be specific targets like religious privilege, the removal of religion from schools, the halting of state support for denominational schools, the abolition of blasphemy law, and the presentation of religion in the media. The rise of new cults and sects, the burgeoning power of Islam, women's rights, gay rights and the right to control one's own fertility all provide focus for secularist activity. Although some of its traditions lie in working class radicalism, the NSS has always been and continues to be supported by a wide range of people; its robust and trenchant stance is still there and will appeal to some but not all of those wishing to present the position of the unbeliever.

G.W. Foote declared in the first issue of *The Freethinker* that it would 'wage relentless war against Superstition in general, and Christian Superstition in particular'. But he also proclaimed the aim of 'diffusing happiness through the grander circle of humanity'.

The Rationalist Press Association

The Rationalist Press Association has been primarily the publishing wing of the humanist movement in Britain. It started as an alternative movement to the National Secular Society. There was a view among some secularists that the fierce anti-religious position was not intellectually satisfying. Doubt could also be positive. But that is not to say that the aim of providing an honest alternative to the religious world view was not carried out assiduously. Rationalists were particularly concerned with promoting the scientific perspective as it undermined religious belief.

Charles Watts was a secularist orator who differed with Bradlaugh and went to lecture in Toronto, having been – together with Austin Holyoake – a printer. His son Charles Albert Watts was brought up as an apprentice in the printing company. He thus learnt the craft and the business of printing at an early age. He had early contact with secularists such as George Holyoake and James Thomson (the poet and essayist). His training was important in the eventual success of the Rationalist Press Association. Charles Albert Watts took over the publishing company, which he was to mould for the next fifty years.

In 1885 he launched a new monthly periodical, *The Agnostic* which did not last the year out. He then hit upon the idea of producing a journal which would keep people in touch with new and sceptical ideas. He started *Watts's Literary Guide* which has survived through several name changes and distinct change in style as the *New Humanist* still published today. It was subtitled 'A Record of Liberal and Advanced publications' and consisted essentially of reviews and summaries of current books and events on secularist themes and ideas. Also in 1885 he began *The Agnostic Annual* which was to survive as *The Rationalist Annual* then as *Question* from 1969 – 1980. A commentator on the former journal of his father, *The Secular Review*, wrote that 'it is the moderation, fairmindedness, and absence of abuse which 1 have noticed in Mr. Watts that cause me to be a subscriber to his paper.' Some complained in the late nineteenth century of 'reverend agnosticism', but the position was to gain greater acceptance for the humanist intellectual position.

Charles Albert Watts had no capital for his publishing projects and established an appeal for at least £1000 to establish a Propaganda Press Fund. It aimed 'to assist in securing the amendment of the law which sanctions the confiscation of property left for anti-theological purposes, and to promote the issuing, advertising, and circulation of publications devoted to 'Freethought and Advanced Religious Reform'. In 1893 its name changed to The Rationalist Press Committee. C. A. Watts aimed to rival the Society for Promoting Christian Knowledge in the breadth of their readership. In 1899 the name changed to the Rationalist Press Association, which was registered as a limited company on 26 May, 1899.

The definition of rationalism as given in the Memorandum of Association was: 'Rationalism is the mental attitude which unreservedly accepts the supremacy of reason and aims at establishing a system of philosophy and ethics verifiable by experience and independent of all arbitrary assumption or authority.' That remains the position today, with the qualification that reason may not be all in the aesthetic and emotional life. The keynote of rationalism was to be the importance of reason and science. The RPA has always avoided a political perspective, but although it has had supporters of all political persuasions, there has always been a tendency towards the liberal and socialist side.

One of Charles Watts' prime aims was to spread knowledge and understanding to the masses. There was a newly educated generation ripe for such knowledge. He wrote that 'in order that truth may prevail in the world at large, it needs that the ignorant shall be taught, that the apathetic shall be aroused, that myths shall be analysed, sophisms exposed, and irrational dogmas refuted.' The first publication was *The Religion of the Twentieth Century* by Joseph McCabe, an ex-Jesuit, whose criticism of religion was very strong. In the second year they published two books by J. M. Robertson, a polymath and politician, who developed a long association with the RPA. Also published was Joseph McCabe's translation of Haeckel's *Riddle of the Universe*.

In the twentieth century an early equivalent of the book club was started. Members of the RPA were entitled to receive books to the value of their subscriptions. This mail order approach was partly to circumscribe the bookshops who thought it inexpedient to sell such heterodox works. The RPA established a series of cheap reprints, the first being Huxley's *Essays and Lectures*, which sold 45,000 in 1902. Charles Albert Watts had an excellent business and publishing flair and the cheap reprints were the RPA's first big success.

Later came the series by which the Association was to become known on a worldwide scale: The Thinker's Library started in 1929. The first four volumes were H. G. Wells's *First and Last Things*, Herbert Spencer's *Education*, Haeckel's *Riddle of the Universe*, and Bradlaugh's *Humanity's Gain from Unbelief*: they sold 300,000 within two years. By the end of the Second World War there were 140 titles. They captured the market for knowledge and ideas in the pre-paperback, pre-television age. It is common still to meet older people who say, 'I first got my humanist ideas from the Thinker's Library.'

Unfortunately, after 1945 the market was overtaken by the paperback revolution and although the RPA has continued to publish books up to this day, the level of activity is comparatively modest and – alas the mainstream market has been lost.

The RPA from its inception appointed Honorary Associates, who gave lustre to the enterprise. In the early days these included Sir Leslie Stephen, Emile Zola, Arnold Bennett, G. M. Trevelyan, Bertrand Russell, H. G. Wells, Albert Einstein, Somerset Maugham and Sigmund Freud. The list remains to this day and includes Colin Blakemore, Richard Dawkins, Michael Foot, and Noam Chomsky.

Among the other activities over the years have been dinners with distinguished speakers, and conferences. Public meetings were held and Honorary Local Secretaries were appointed to enroll new members and in some cases to start local groups. The network of local humanist groups has its origin partly in this activity.

Although not largely an organisation campaigning on specific issues, two areas were of particular interest to the RPA: the domination of the BBC by Christian propaganda and the need to provide secular education. Under Reith the early B.B.C. was a place for the transmission of Christianity rather than debate about religion, especially on a Sunday. On October 15, 1946 the Chairman of the Governors and the Director General of the B.B.C. received a delegation from the RPA and rationalists came to take part in some discussions on religion. However, to this day there is dissatisfaction at the privileged position of religion in the media.

There was rationalist activity in the first decade of the twentieth century to try and ensure that secular instruction alone should be given in publicly funded schools. The issue became important again during the Second World War when the Coalition Govermnent prepared an Education Bill to widen the benefits of education. The plans included a daily act of worship and religious instruction according to an agreed syllabus. To this day the question of religion in schools much exercises humanists.

In its heyday the RPA played a significant part in changing and secularising the views of educated people in a period of great change. Perhaps the task became more difficult once theologians were undermining theology, scientists were common in the media, and mainstream publishing contained many books of a sceptical tenor. Yet, the RPA continues to function today, mainly as a publishing organisation, but also in interventions in the media.

South Place Ethical Society

The National Secular Society and Rationalist Press Association were largely formed in opposition to religion; the South Place Ethical Society arose from the heart of religion and was transmuted into ethical humanism. A related Ethical Movement acquired an independent existence and eventually becamee the British Humanist Association.

The origin was a non-conformist chapel started in Bishopsgate in 1793. It was Universalist – that is it did not believe in hell, but rather that all may be saved. Its first minister was an American, Elhanan Winchester, a pioneer of the Universalist faith. He wrote tracts on Universalism and penned a reply to Thomas Paine's *The Age of Reason*; he saw the French revolution as a prelude to the end of the world. In 1794 he returned to the USA under pressure from his fifth wife.

William Vidler took over and he advanced from Universalism to Unitarianism, that is the belief that the so-called trinity were in fact one. He remained there until 1814, when age and health forced him to retire two years before his death. He was admired for his sermons and his conversation, and when he died an eloquent young man was ready to succeed: William James Fox.

Fox was an East Anglian who had been involved in radical movements as a young man. He helped to organise a group of radical weavers in Norwich into a branch of the London Corresponding Society, which had sympathy with the French Revolution. He studied theology at Homerton Independent College and became a Unitarian minister in Fareham. A friend, Peter Taylor, who was a Leicester MP, became his benefactor. On the death of William Vidler he was invited to become minister to the Bishopsgate chapel in 1817.

His congregation became aware of his political radicalism when he delivered a speech from the pulpit against the imprisonment of Carlile for reprinting *The Age of Reason*. He also supported universal education. His congregation grew and they decided on a move from Bishopsgate to Finsbury, the foundation of a new chapel being laid in 1823. At the inauguration of the Finsbury Unitarian Chapel the next year, Fox dedicated it to the worship of virtue and freedom – very wide aims for a Unitarian body. There were soon eminent speakers at the chapel as Finsbury was becoming a prosperous area and South Place developed a well-to-do congregation which was increasingly known in London's intellectual and religious life. J. S. Mill wrote: 'Fox's religion was what the religion of all would be if we were in a healthy state; a religion of spirit, not of dogma, and Catholic in the best sense.' Fox campaigned for abolition of the Test Acts and Emancipation of the Catholics – consistent with his belief in religious freedom.

He was a highly successful journalist, writing frequently for the Unitarian journal the *Monthly Repository* becoming its editor in due course. Contributors included J. S. Mill and Harriet Martineau. He published some of Browning's early poems. After a scandal resulting from a liaison with a member of his congregation, he moved away from unitarianism and became very active as a journalist. He campaigned vigorously for the anti-corn-law league and became well-known as a political speaker. In 1847 he became a member of Parliament and sought release from his South Place activities. A number of assistant ministers were appointed, but none with great success. The chapel went through an uncertain period. But in 1863 a young American was appointed for a six month trial period: Moncure Conway.

Conway was born in Virginia in 1832. He was deeply influenced by the ideas and example of Emerson. He was trained as a Methodist Preacher, but moved to Unitarianism. He supported the cause of negro emancipation, although his family owned slaves. He was deeply troubled during the Civil War and came to England to argue the emancipation cause.

Once established at the Unitarian Chapel, he slowly made changes in practice and outlook. He changed the practice of always having a biblical reading, introducing other texts such as sacred works from the east. He decided he could not offer prayer and offered a meditation instead. He was interested in world religions and anthropology. He had a high regard for science and was friendly with T.H. Huxley and Charles Lyell, the geologist, who sometimes attended the chapel. He also fought for state education. His lectures were extended during the week and the chapel became partly a centre of adult education. The volume of *Hymns and Anthems* created by the Flower sisters, was widely used. It was changed at South Place to the more agnostic *Hymns of Modern Thought*. A book of ethical scriptures produced by Conway, *The Sacred Anthology* became a best seller.

In 1882, in his fiftieth year, he decided on a long trip back to the US. Two years later he decided that he would leave the chapel for good and made his farewells in 1885. With no clear leader, the chapel relied more and more on outside speakers. In 1887, Conway suggested that Stanton Coit, a young American active in the ethical movement, would be suitable to lead South Place. He held the position for some years.

Conway returned to London in 1892. He published his *Life of Thomas Paine*, the first major work to provide a positive image of Paine. But in 1897, he decided, largely because of the poor health of his wife, that he would make his final departure. He died in Paris ten years later.

In the twentieth century, failing to find a significant leader, SPES came to rely on a system of Appointed Lecturers. The subjects became largely topical. Leading speakers were J. M. Robertson, Joseph McCabe, and J. A. Hobbes. The chapel was much in demand as a centre for protest during the Boer Wars. The decision to move from Finsbury, on account of the decay of the building, was made in 1913. In 1927 Conway Hall was opened in Red Lion Square. It became famous for its chamber concerts on Sunday evenings, which continue until this day. It has remained as a Sunday morning meeting place, with a small group of controversialists, and continuing adherence to ethical principles. The *Ethical Record* is a monthly journal which mainly reports lectures. SPES maintains a library with valuable archives and some new books on science and ethics. Its finances are sustained by letting out the hall and rooms to other organisations – a policy of free speech allows a very wide range of political, artistic, and religious groups to meet there. The use for religious meetings is controversial.

At the centenary of South Place Ethical Society Conway concluded an address with the words:

> Brothers, this temple has hidden foundations – in human needs, in your love of truth and freedom, and of each other; in your hope and courage; in your humanity, your helpfulness, your sympathy: let these deep foundations remain, and this Society will never fail.

Over a hundred years later, SPES tries to maintain and promote these ideals.

British Humanist Association

The British Humanist Association arose out of the Ethical Societies which were founded in the late nineteenth century. The London Ethical Society was founded in 1886 and attracted supporters such as Henry Sidgwick and Leslie Stephen. By 1906 there were 42 Ethical Societies in Britain. They held an idealistic philosophic position and were concerned with moral development and social improvement. They took the form of a debating group with a helping of moral earnestness and a touch of residual ritual.

They owed much to the American leader of the Ethical Culture movement, Felix Adler. He was concerned that those who abandoned religion did not abandon moral duty. He felt that Sunday morning meetings with addresses and music could sustain people: 'It is an unspeakable comfort to meet there others who are trying to surmount the difficulties of life in the ethical spirit.'

One of Adler's assistants in the New York Ethical Society, Stanton Coit, was born in Ohio in 1857 and his mother was a spiritualist. This gave the experience of identification with unorthodox belief, which had a a long-term influence on him. He became a sceptic at the age of 17, while studying at Amherst. He became the only non-religious lecturer there, admired for his being 'the most sceptical man in our class but also the most spiritual.' He was steeped in the moral idealism of Emerson and was later much influenced by Kant's idealism when he studied in Germany.

He returned to the US from Germany via London and spent three months joining in the educational and social work in the slums, organised at Toynbee

Hall. Coit developed an amalgam of idealism, social inspiration and ethical socialism which was to last his life.

After the first resignation of Moncure Conway at South Place Ethical Society he took up a post as leader there. He wanted to make SPES a part of the Ethical movement, but he fell out with its members, particularly over his attempts to elaborate the rituals there. He founded philanthropic groups and ethical classes, but resigned after seven years in 1891.

He transferred his energies to the ethical societies, lecturing very widely and becoming particularly attached to the West London Ethical Society; it later became known as the Ethical Church, Bayswater. He built up a following that was impressed by music, ardent literature and inspiring addresses.

Coit developed extremely ambitious ideas, expressed in his two books *National Idealism and a State Church* and *National Idealism and the Book of Common Prayer*. He had a vision of the principles and practices of the ethical societies/churches becoming part of the Church of England. He wanted a public expression of the moral ideal, which could be objectified and celebrated. But all this involved a wild lack of comprehension of the Church of England. He wrote on Ethical Democracy in 1937 outlining his belief in the expression of morality throughout 'the entire life of a democratic community'. He died in 1944 having had much influence, but little success in putting his ideas into practice. Some of his ideas remain as a legacy to the BHA: the idea of working together with religious groups, the desire to put moral principles into practice in social work, the adherence to democratic principles and the 'open society'.

Coit had formed the union of Ethical Societies and edited *The Ethical World*. A decade after his death there were moves to bring together the separate humanist organisations. In 1950 a Humanist Council was formed 'as a liaison committee to link the Rationalist Press Association, the Ethical Union and South Place Ethical Society', which was not at that time affiliated to the Ethical Union. There developed a hope for a merger between the Ethical Union and the Rationalist Press Association. The word 'humanist' was increasingly used to describe adherents' views in these organisations. In 1957 an interim Humanist Association was formed between the Ethical Union and the RPA. It embarked on many joint enterprises including attempts to gain more hearing in the broadcasting media, support for Freedom from Hunger, support for a school in Botswana.

A further attempt at merger was made in 1962, relative wealth and charitable status causing difficulties, but the link remained for five years. The new British Humanist Association gained members and increased activities, having been launched with a dinner in May 1963 at which A. J. Ayer and Baroness Wootton were speakers. The BHA set up sub-groups such as the Humanist Committee on Moral and Religious Education, the Humanist Counselling Service, Humanist Holidays, the Humanist Housing Association and the Humanist Teachers Association. The flow of social reform in the 1960s coincided with this surge of humanist activity.

The BHA has remained an organisation with qualities relating to social consciousness and social action as much as criticism of religion, although seeing as important issues such as religious privilege, the inequitable treatment of humanist views by the media and fair teaching about religion and morality in schools. Harold Blackham, its first Director, wrote: 'Persons and groups of different faiths would have institutions in common for general social purposes....' With echoes of Coit, the BHA have been particularly successful in establishing a network of officiants for humanist ceremonies – funerals, weddings, naming ceremonies, and gay and lesbian affirmation ceremonies. They have also run successful annual conferences covering intellectual issues of the day and also offering workshops on humanist activities. A network of humanist groups, the legacy of both ethical societies and secularist groups, provide local presence and fellowship.

The delegates from four London ethical societies met in 1895 to form a federation. Their aims were: 'By purely natural and human means to assist individual and social efforts after right living' . All the humanist organisations today would probably accept that as an underlying aim.

Two further humanist organisations need to be mentioned briefly: The Gay and Lesbian Humanist Association and the International Humanist and Ethical Union.

Gay and Lesbian Humanist Association

The Gay and Lesbian Humanist Association was founded in 1979. Its aim was to increase understanding of homosexuality among humanists and to further understanding of humanism among homosexuals. It has campaigned vigorously for gay and lesbian rights, such as an equal age of consent with heterosexuals and the right for gays and lesbians to openly enter the military (now achieved). A remaining aim is the right for legally sanctioned partnership between same sex couples. It offers assistance with gay and lesbian affirmations and provides support and friendship among humanist homosexuals.

The International and Ethical Union

The earliest attempt at international co-operation between humanist groups came with the World Union of Freethinkers. Bradlaugh, who had co-operated with Mazzini, took a keen role in the foundation of the WUF. It began in the

1880s as a federation of international freethought groups, known both as the Freethought Federation and the Brussels Federation. International Congresses were held and there was support for the defence of Ferrer, the Spanish educationalist who successfully founded secular, progressive schools and was executed (1909) on a trumped up charge.

WUF was active in the 1930s. Bradlaugb Bonner wrote in the *Freethinker*:

> The formation of the Union of Freethinkers has fluttered more than one dovecote. It has led in Poland to the prohibition of freethought associations. In Holland and Belgium the Catholic newspapers have hurled at it a stream of abuse, endeavouring to curdle the blood of their readers. ... In Italy, Germany, Austria, Poland, Roumania, Lithuania, Latvia, Estonia, and Bulgaria, Freethought is banned. Yet the Pansy grows hidden in secret places despite the Crutched Cross, the Swastika and the Axe.

(The pansy became a symbol of freethought, perhaps in association with the word *pensée*.)

Freethinkers were persecuted by the Nazis. The movement collapsed during the Second World War. There was difficulty in reviving it and in the decade after the war Harold Blackham and Jap van Praag came to the conclusion that it was beyond revival. Representing the Ethical Union and Dutch Humanist League they started the International Humanist and Ethical Union in 1952. The founder members were also the American Ethical Union, the Freireligiöse Gemeinden Deutschland, the Humanistichse Verbund van Nederland en Belgie and the Indian Radical Humanist Movement. Julian Huxley presided over their first conference in Amsterdam. An opening conference listed five 'fundamentals of ethical humanism': being democratic, seeking to use science creatively rather than destructively, being ethical, insisting that personal liberty is an end that must be combined with social responsibility, and being a way of life.' It has expanded to nearly 100 member organisations across the world and is represented at international meetings, holds regular conferences, produces a quarterly magazine, and campaigns on a wide range of issues, such as human values, economic justice across the world, freedom of religion and from religion. It now sees a major part of its task as developing humanism across the third world.

The IHEU is in the forefront of developing a global humanism, with the ideal that humanist values may arise throughout the world.

11 *International Humanism*

'My country is the world and my religion to do good.' This epigram by Thomas Paine encapsulates what humanists feel about the world. Any complete and balanced view of humanism has an international dimension. We differ in the extent to which we have travelled or in our ability to empathise with other parts of the world, but the global element of humanism is undeniable. It was well put by the Nigerian playwright, Wole Soyinka: 'My allegiance is to man. Locally to the Nigerians; universally to humanity.'

Humanists want to do what can be done – sometimes very little – for those imprisoned unjustly and without due trial for their beliefs and writings. Of course, there will be especial concern for those mistreated because of their criticism of religion, such as Taslima Nasrin from Bangla Desh, who was forced out of the country because of her alleged criticism of Islam. Humanists , of course, also extend their concern to those attacked for their religious beliefs. There are many specific organisations such as Amnesty International or Index on Censorship dealing with these issues and humanists support them. Humanists will especially concern themselves with those pursued for their humanist beliefs, such as Dr Younus Shaikh persecuted in Pakistan for alleged blasphemy.

Globalisation is now a much-used word. It can be used in a positive and negative sense. Globalisation can refer to the fact that human beings throughout the world are interlinked, by electronic technology, by easy travel, by international news systems, by international trade, by international cultural exchanges (although these are not available to the greater part of the world). It is possible if you want to (but many do not!) to know within moments about the latest flood in northern India, the election in Yugoslavia, the conflict in Sierra Leone, the famine in Ethiopia, the latest execution in Texas and so on. (Well, news is usually bad, almost by definition.) Such knowledge can engender sympathy and understanding which is necessary for a global perspective.

Globalisation can also refer to the international trade and financial system, which effectively delays third world economic development and increases the division between the wealthy North and the poor South. The indebtedness of most Southern countries sometimes outweighs the aid given by affluent countries. Attempts, with Britain playing a prominent role, to cancel debts, have been very slow in taking effect. The power of international corporations is often seen as another brake on developing countries: they control prices, monopolise markets, and prevent the growth of indigenous production and local trade. There has been much protest about these factors at international meetings and many humanists would be behind, or among, the protesters.

The humanist perspective has been a worldwide phenomenon from ancient to modern times. There is evidence within early religions of scepticism: it can take the form of highlighting the transience of life, doubt about what lies beyond, and emphasis on enjoying the present life. These thoughts were found in early writings in Mesopotamia and ancient Egypt.

In India doubt is found in the Sanskrit scriptures. The Śvetāśvatara Upaniṣad contains the lines:

> Is Brahma the cause? Whence are we born?
> Whereby do we live, and whither do we go?
>
> Should time, or nature, or necessity, or chance,
> or the elements be considered as the cause,
> or he who is called the person?

This is a questioning of the first cause, such as you might find in philosophy in recent centuries in Europe.

The Cārvakā school of thought within Hinduism in the sixth century B. C. had a completely naturalistic view of the universe and a practical and hedonistic view of ethics. In the Sarva-siddhanta-samgraha are the words:

> Only the perceived exists; the unperceivable does not exist, by reason of its never having been perceived;
> While life remains let a man live happily, let him feed on ghee [butter] though he runs into debts;
> When once the body has become ashes, how can it ever return again?

The most naturalistic approach in ancient thought is found in China. Confucius (c551 – 479BC) laid down a tradition of this-worldly ethics. He is reported as answering the question 'What is wisdom?': 'To give oneself earnestly to securing righteousness and justice among the people, and while respecting the gods and demons, to keep aloof from them, that may be called wisdom.'

Lao Tzu, who lived at some time between 480 and 222BC developed a pantheistic naturalism with emphasis on the search for peace of mind. Both Taoism and Confucianism later developed more superstitious elements.

A truly sceptical Chinese thinker was Wang Ch'ung (27–97AD), who has been called the Lucretius of China. He stressed the use of reason and criticised anthropomorphism, suggesting that man's life on earth was like lice living in the folds of a garment. In a passage considering 'spirits' and 'sacrifices' he concludes 'man has his happiness in his own hands, and the spirits have nothing to do with it. It depends on his virtues and not on sacrifices.'

As can be seen it is a mistake to consider humanism just as a European outlook. The development of humanism in modern India and in the USA today demonstrates the vigour in the humanist vision. Both countries have a secular state floating on a sea of religion. The predominant Hinduism and powerful Islam in India are the backdrop before which humanists must work. They have the advantage that India is – technically – a secular state. In the US Christianity is very powerful and as the polls show the level of religious belief is much higher than in Europe. While some liberal religious groups such as the Unitarians may be close to humanism, the forceful evangelical Right provides a formidable challenge for humanists.

India has one of the strongest humanist movements in the developing world. There are four main organisations: the Indian Secular Society, the Atheist Centre, the Radical Humanist Association and the Indian Rationalist Association. All the organisations are concerned to keep India a secular state as declared in the Constitution, despite moves by Hindutva nationalists to weaken this concept. The secular state arose from the need to deal with religious conflict known as communalism, that is religious strife. Riots between Hindus and Muslims are not uncommon and there has been some persecution of Christians by Hindu extremists. The recent rise of Hindu nationalism, the *Hindutva*, has had a damaging effect on the relationship between religious groups. The best-known example of communalism was the conflict around the mosque at Ayodhya, which was allegedly on the site of a Hindu temple, the birth place of the Indian god Rama. The mosque was pulled down by a mob. There was no suggestion that the two religions could come to a compromise and the destruction of the mosque at Ayodha remains an appalling example of the intolerance towards each other of religious groups. Even some years after the destruction the conflict was causing riots between Muslims and Hindus.

The Indian Secular Society aims to preserve the secular state and believes that 'the most serious threat to the development of India as a secular democratic state, guaranteeing individual freedom and social justice to its citizens, comes from religious obscurantism and cultural activities for the promotion of its aims'. The Indian Secular Society was founded by Professor A. B. Shah, who was an expert on the Islamic religion. He campaigned for a Uniform Civil Code: the Personal Laws in India allowing different legal codes on, for instance, marriage, for different religions were not acceptable – all religions should be treated alike. The Indian Secular Society has also campaigned against the Hindu taboo on cow slaughter, arguing that it has no basis in the Hindu scriptures.

The Indian Radical Humanist Association aims to change society and politics. They provide a powerful humanist intellectual current in present-day Indian culture. They want to bring about change for ordinary people in India:

> To make people conscious of the urge to freedom, encourage their self-reliance and awaken in them the sense of individual dignity, inculcate the value of rationalism and secular morality, and spread the spirit of cosmopolitan Humanism, by showing the people the way to solve their daily problems by popular initiative. The Radical Humanists will combat ignorance, fatalism, blind faith and the sense of individual hopelessness, which are the basis of authoritarianism. They will put all the social traditions and institutions to the test of the humanistic outlook.

This ambitious perspective originated in the ideas of M. N. Roy (1887 – 1954). He was a freedom fighter from Bengal working to overthrow British rule at the beginning of the 20th century. Under threat of arrest he escaped to America, where he spent much time in the library at New York. In Mexico, he founded the first communist party outside Russia. He went to Moscow, where he worked with the leaders before the totalitarianism of Stalin had become apparent. He left just in time and returned to India, where he knew he was likely to be imprisoned by the British. In prison he studied and thought a great deal and relinquished Marxism for his own brand of humanism. He was active in politics but disbanded the political party he founded – in favour of direct action and grass roots politics.

Among the direct action undertaken by individual radical humanists is the Streehitkarini, an organisation founded by Indumati Parikh for health and birth control information for women in the slums of Mumbai. The work is extremely successful on a micro-level, but could be seen as a drop in the ocean in the vastly expanding homeless population of Mumbai.

Humanism in practice is conducted with great energy at the Atheist Centre, in Vijayawada, Southern India. The centre was founded by Gora (1902 – 1975) and his wife Saraswati Gora, aiming to give education and social support to all people, including the lowest castes. He was influenced by Gandhi in his belief in the power of direct action. His overt atheism led him into difficulties in the colleges where he lectured on biology. He started the Centre with the aim of putting what he called 'positive atheism' into practice. Run largely by his extended family, the activities have grown greatly since the inception of the centre.

The Association for Economic Equality, which originated in the Atheist Centre's rural work is now an independent organisation with support from Save the Children Fund and Oxfam. It has a hospital and training in rural skills and self-sufficiency – with the aim of improving village life and helping to stem the flow of people to the overcrowded cities. At the Centre itself there is a women's hostel, for mistreated women, where they learn skills that can lead to independence. There is also atheist propaganda, with a printing press and a regular monthly magazine. The Gora Science Centre gives education in scientific methods. There have been campaigns to rescue child temple prostitutes and to rehabilitate criminals. There have also been anti-superstition campaigns in the region.

There are secular weddings – with vegetables rather than flowers, since growth of flowers is seen (rather puritanically) as waste of land use. As part of the humanist education they hold pork and beef suppers at which religious taboos can be defied, and fire-walking demonstrations to show that religious powers are not needed to perform this display.

In a country where the godmen and gurus are still rife, anti-superstition campaigning is very necessary. B. Premenand, Convenor of the Indian Committee for the Scientific Investigation of the Paranormal (CSICOP) and editor of the *Indian Skeptic*, takes the lead in demonstrating throughout the country the science underlying the 'magical' tricks.

The Indian Rationalist Association is an effective campaigning organisation, particularly criticising superstitious events – such as statues of Ganesh drinking milk, tears dropping from the virgin's eye, and the mass hysteria at an alleged 'monkey man'. It is also a vigorous publishing organisation, with books in several languages and selling particularly well in Kerala, a Southern state that has a high level of literacy.

In the twentieth century there are strong strands of humanism in India. Although Gandhi remained a deist, his direct action, determination to end casteism, and belief that members of different religions should live together influenced humanists. Among the imaginative writers, whose works have a humanist tendency are the great poet and playwright, Tagore, and more recently novelists such as Anita Desai, Amit Chaudhuri and Rohinton Mistry. Salman Rushdie has become such a *cause célèbre* that the imaginativeness and linguistic vibrance of his novels are sometimes forgotten. His novels address a key twentieth century experience – a sense of identity in a multicultural world. Although the dismay of some Muslims with *Satanic Verses* may be understood, the desire to destroy Rushdie for his writings has been deplored by humanists everywhere. The combination of religious and political power can be very dangerous.

In the US the principle of separation of Church and State has been established in reaction to the religious persecution which the migrants fled from in England and this serves to control the sectarian disputes of a very forceful Christian presence. The principle of separation is notably applied to schools, where it is forbidden to introduce religion, either in the form of worship or in the form of religious instruction. Religious groups have been pressing at the margins by trying to introduce religious activity as a voluntary activity out of official school hours. The teaching of evolution in science lessons has been challenged in court by evangelicals. In Kansas campaigners have succeeded in having evolution science banned from schools. Christian groups have suggested unsuccessfully that humanism is a religion and that evolution as a 'tenet' of this 'religion' should not be presented in schools. Another issue dividing humanists and many religious groups as elsewhere in the world is abortion – where humanists argue for the right of a woman to choose abortion.

In public life, to admit to atheism would be political death. Any candidate for President has to flag up his religious beliefs – yet the third President, Jefferson was a sceptical deist, who stated 'Reason and free inquiry are the only effectual agents against error.' Statistics show a much higher rate of belief in God and church attendance than in Europe. There was a strong religious element in the persecution of President Clinton for his sexual peccadillos.

Humanists are charged with responsibility for the rise of crime, satanic abuse, and the breakup of families. There is, therefore, considerable need for a humanist voice in the US. There are three main organisations: the American Humanists, the Council for Secular Humanism and the American Atheists. A number of Ethical Societies complete the humanist spectrum.

The American Atheist Association concentrates its efforts on the privileges of religious groups and the lack of rights for atheists. *The American Atheist Newsletter* reports campaigns such as the law suit to remove the phrase 'in God We Trust' from the US currency, to stop prayers in public institutions, and to prohibit the display of religious symbols in public buildings.

The Council for Secular Humanism produces the journal *Free Inquiry*, one of the highest quality humanist journals in the world. Its aims are 'to promote and nurture the good life – life guided by reason and science, freed from the dogmas of God and State, inspired by compassion for fellow humans, and driven by the ideals of human freedom, happiness and understanding'. The associated organisation Prometheus Books is the foremost humanist publisher in the world. Philosopher Professor Paul Kurtz is a leading writer and entrepreneur in these organisations. Under his guidance the Council for Secular Humanism has built the Center for Inquiry, one of the most impressive centres for humanism in the world.

The American Humanist Association publishes *The Humanist* and campaigns on broad human rights issues as well as religious controversies.

The Canadian Humanist Association publishes *Humanist in Canada* and prints prominently in one of its issues: 'Man's chief purpose . . . is the creation and preservation of values: that is what gives meaning to our civilisation and the participation in this is what gives significance, ultimately, to the individual human life.'

Australia is a very secular society, with a number of humanist groups. There is a federation of humanist societies acting as an umbrella organisation for separate humanist societies in most Australian States. There is also the Rationalist Association of Australia with its associated Humanist Society of Australia. The two main journals are *The Australian Rationalist* and *The Australian Humanist*. The Rationalist Society of New Zealand is also active.

In Australia humanist organisations have been involved with human rights issues such as reconciliation with the indigenous aborigines and the rights of refugees and asylum seekers. Other familiar humanist causes are the right to voluntary euthanasia and gay rights. There has been a vigorous campaign to have the religious question in the census changed so that in answer to the question 'What is your religion?' the reply 'None' should come first.

Humanist organisations in Europe vary greatly in their size, energy and scope. There is a distinct difference between the humanist organisations in Protestant countries and the anti-clerical movements in Catholic countries. Humanism in Eastern Europe has its own problems, especially the past link between atheism and communism. The extent to which they have influence in their countries relates to membership, individual leaders and above all their sources of financial support.

The largest European humanist organisation in ratio to the size of population is the Norwegian Humanist Association. They have over 50,000 members and are steadily growing. They attribute much of their success to the humanist coming-of-age ceremony, which has great family and cultural importance in Norwegian life. The ceremonies, which are preceded by some education in moral values, enable the non-religious to celebrate the occasion in a rich and dignified way. Many people encounter humanism in this way and it is a prime source of support for their organisation. Weddings and funerals are also carried out extensively by Norwegian humanists as they are in many other European countries.

The Lutheran Church remains influential in Norway. Nevertheless there is also a distinct freethought tradition with the writers Ibsen, Strindberg, Bjørn Bjørnsen and Nansen, the explorer.

Norwegian humanists are also concerned with education and with the recent law that insists on Christian Education in schools; they join with non-Christian religions in opposing this law and are bringing a court case on the right of the child not to receive religious indoctrination. The Norwegian Humanist Association has impressive headquarters, very-well produced publications, and has had excellent leadership in recent years.

Humanism is also a powerful force in the Netherlands. There is a longstanding tradition of tolerance stretching back to openness to Huguenot refugees from France in the seventeenth century (including the great sceptic Pierre Bayle). Thinkers such as the renaissance humanist Erasmus, and the pantheist philosopher Spinoza, who wrote *Ethics* in the seventeenth century, have marked Dutch culture.

The Humanistisch Verbond, founded in 1946, was guided by the Dutch philosopher Jaap van Praag during its early decades. The modern organisation deals with human rights issues in the broadest sense and has looked at the situation of asylum seekers, racism, intolerance and bioethical problems. They have led the campaign to legalise a controlled form of voluntary euthanasia and have supported the move to legalise relationships between gays and lesbians.

Another Dutch humanist organisation, Humanitas, offers an alternative to the charitable work of the churches. It is a highly professional organisation, with state support, involved in such areas as rehabilitation of prisoners, child care and the problems of the elderly. The principle of state support for activities parallel to those of the churches has enabled much humanist activity to take place. The Humanist Broadcasting organisation, Humanistische Omroep, receives money from the Ministry of Education, Culture and Sciences. They have the right to broadcast 39 hours per year of television and 250 hours per year of radio.

The University of Humanist Studies is likewise supported by the state. The University offers academic and professional training; as well as philosophy, sociology and ethics; part of their course is practical work in counselling.

Public funds also support humanism in Belgium. The two distinct regions, the Flemish and the French-speaking, have separate organisations and activities. The Flemish-based Humanistisch Verbond has 80 local groups and is concerned with independence of thought, human dignity and social responsibility. Other Flemish organisations offer moral counselling and train teachers of ethics.

The Centre d'Action Laïque, in French-speaking Belgium, has a network of social groups, regular publications, including the journal, *Espace de Liberté*, and a large headquarters. Their work includes counselling, general information, secular ceremonies, and ethical study. In both regions of Belgium there are 'Houses for Secularism' which are local centres functioning as a focus for humanism.

The word 'laïcite' is very important for French humanism. The word means 'secularism', but has implications of a totally lay society, which is stronger than 'secularism'. The words 'libre penseur' and 'rationaliste' are used more than 'humaniste' in France. France has an impressive sceptical tradition from Montaigne to Voltaire and Diderot and on to Sartre and Camus. Likewise, Italy has a more anti-clerical movement than a humanist movement. Such anti-clerical movements tended to have a strong socialist agenda. In Italy the Giordano Bruno association remembers the persecution of this heretic and continues with anti-clerical campaigning. Freethought in Italy can be found in the views of the fighter for Unification, Garibaldi, who had contact with Charles Bradlaugh. The composer Verdi, even though he wrote a dramatic and dramatically successful Mass, was an atheist. Modern writers such as the Holocaust survivor Primo Levi, and the novelists, Umberto Eco and Calvino, have humanist elements in their work. For an Italian freethinker the presence of the Vatican must be a permanent reminder of religious power and misuse of power.

Germany, too, has writers essential to the humanist tradition: in the nineteenth century the poet Heine and playwright, Georg Büchner were key sceptics. The new German Biblical criticism in the nineteenth century from those such as David Friedrich Strauss had an impact worldwide, and the sociologists of religion such as Feuerbach, who saw that religion was a social construct, were equally important.

The German Humanist Association is kept on a sound financial basis by the national system of a Church tax. All citizens are obliged to pay a tax to their churches; but non-believers can direct their tax to a German humanist association. An essential part of their activity is the ethical teaching in schools, which particularly continues in the former East Germany. German humanists are also concerned with race relations, especially in relation to immigrants and 'guest' workers, and with neo-Nazism.

In the former communist states of eastern Europe, there are small nascent humanist groups. Poland has the problem of the longstanding Catholic power – given an impetus by a Polish pope and by the recrudescence of Catholic churches at the end of communist rule. Threats to the right to abortion and to gay rights have come from the Catholic Church, as have attempts to enforce religious education in schools. There are small humanist groups in Romania and Hungary. There is a Humanist Association in Russia which is largely an academic organisation. The problems of daily life in Russia are so great, that there are difficulties in finding the energy to promote humanism. Nevertheless, small groups of humanists provide a still voice of reason in a sea of chaos.

Two continents are sadly missing in this survey: South America and Africa. There are small humanist groups in Mexico and Argentina, but the continent as a whole does not have a formal humanist presence – although there are writers such as Borges and Gabriel García Márquez. There are a number of humanist individuals in Africa who act as a focus for humanist thought, but there is no well-organised humanist movement. The problems of Africa are enormous, the AIDS epidemic, drought, wars and civil wars, but if humanism is a philosophy for the world it ought to be possible to contribute something positive to the problems of Africa.

Looking at humanism across the world, we can see the need to develop strategies to deal with the various forms of fundamentalism and the need for humanism to develop an ethical content as well as a counter-religious one, humanists must work with other international organisations, such as Oxfam or Amnesty International. Also the much criticised United Nations needs support and, indeed, the International Humanist and Ethical Union is ensuring that there is a presence in some of the Non Governmental Organisations of the UN. There is need to support democracy, free speech, freedom of thought and scientific inquiry: humanists assert that these are universal concepts and not relative ones, although there are recent challenges to this view.

Globalisation as seen in the hegemonic financial, political and trading dominance of the industrial countries needs challenging. Globalisation as a perception that the world is one should be embraced by humanists.

The Indian integrationist Swami Rama Tirtha said: 'The whole world is one home and all are family members.' In E. M. Forster's novel *A Passage to India*, the character Fielding says: 'the world is a globe of men trying to reach each other' who ' can best do so by the help of good will plus culture and intelligence'.

12

Humanist Action and Humanist Living

In what direction does humanism impel people to action? In what ways does humanism guide and inspire people to live a fulfilled life? These two questions are crucial to the role of humanism as a philosophy of life.

Since humanism insists that we are grounded in this world and in this moment of time, humanists want to do something to make their society and their individual lives more bearable. They will vary enormously in how far they wish to be political or social activists, but most will see the importance of playing a part in their community. The lives that we achieve for ourselves vary hugely in their satisfaction, because we each start with different personalities and circumstances, but all humanists will see the aim for a full and contented life as important.

Historically humanists have tended to be drawn to areas of social reform: education and especially the teaching of human values, women's rights, the right to control one's fertility, the right to choose when to end one's life, opposition to religious privilege in the law and in the media, freedom of speech and information, the rights of homosexuals, bisexuals and transgendered people, the striving for racial equality. Some of these aims have received humanist attention for the rather negative reason that religious groups have opposed them. Nevertheless they become positive ends if taken in themselves. In some areas humanists will certainly work together with religious groups to bring about change. There are no sets of rules in humanism and not everyone will agree how to make progress in all these areas.

We share with people of many beliefs a broad concern with human rights, eradication of poverty, peaceful resolution of internal and international conflicts, and so on. We will be likely to act within an existing political party or campaigning group to forward such aims. Humanists have tended to support left of centre political parties, believing them more likely to bring about change and to work for the entire population, but there are conservative humanists. The tendency of conservative atheists is not to identify with humanism, because of its reforming ambitions. The Parliamentary Humanist

Group has for years failed to draw any Conservative Members, thus losing some of the facilities given to all-party parliamentary groups.

Research has shown that a large proportion of the small number of signed up humanists are members of, or supporters of, organisations such as Amnesty International, Oxfam, Shelter, and many other charitable organisations. It is often asked why humanists are not seen to be doing charitable work, as with specifically Christian charities. Some believe it would do the public image of humanism much good if there were more visibility in these areas, but humanists see themselves acting for the good of all and see no need to label everything they do as 'humanist'. Humanists do not aim to be a mass movement with a political agenda agreed by all.

There is, however, a humanist agenda which is persistent and in which much progress was made in the last century. Campaigning for freedom of speech and freedom of information, for civil liberties and the right to free debate on religious matters are all humanist ends.

The right to control fertility has been a humanist concern for two hundred years. Freethinkers such as Richard Carlile published information at a time when the mention of birth control was taboo. He was concerned with the effect of persistent pregnancy upon women's health in his *Every Woman's Book or What is Love?* (1825–26) The republication of Knowlton's *The Fruits of Philosophy* in 1887, which gave birth control information, led to the prosecution of Bradlaugh and Annie Besant – they only escaped gaol on a technicality. In the twentieth century many campaigners for birth control were humanists and many churches opposed them. The Catholic Church still does – to little avail in the Western world. The rationale behind humanist support of birth control is twofold: first, the concern for the health of mothers and children; second, the need to balance the size of the world population with our global resources.

A related area is that of a woman's right to have an abortion. Never an easy decision for a woman, the medical help for a safe abortion should be there for those who choose it. All working in the field agree that early abortions are better than late ones – but early abortions are much more likely if information and medical help are easily available. Those who oppose abortion have a fundamentally different attitude to the foetus than humanists. Opponents of abortion seem to lack an understanding of what the foetus is and how many die quite naturally. The humanist sees conception as the potential for life – as are all the potential conjunctions of eggs and sperms – not as the completed life. At what stage the foetus becomes a human being is complex. In fact no one is fully human until born and the process of socialising begins. Early abortions are preferable, because of the development of the foetus and the condition of the mother. Ready availability of professional medical help at an early stage is obviously important.

There are many new areas of bio-medical ethics, which humanists can join in researching and discussing. The possibility of fertilisation by artificial means and the whole host of possibilities arising as a result of genetic research are areas that must be considered seriously by society as a whole. The processes of IVF and cloning present new potentialities and the decoding of the human genome creates vast new possibilities for medical and commercial use of specific genes.

The right to choice and sexual freedom should also be extended to homosexuals. In Britain in the sixties humanists supported the campaign to decriminalise homosexual relations. There was no legal sanction against lesbianism (though much stigma) but gay men could, most inappropriately, be sent to prison for homosexual acts. This led to many blackmail attempts, but even worse caused homosexuals to stifle their feelings and disguise their nature. There has been much change since the 1967 law reform and gays and lesbians are now often able to be open about their sexual orientation. Bisexuals and those undergoing a sex change may be less well understood. The position in many parts of the world remains oppressive for homosexuals, but in some countries, such as the Netherlands, there is legal recognition of homosexual partnerships. The considerable change in the understanding of homosexuals has been supported by humanists.

The right to choose at the end of life is also contentious. If suffering from a terminal illness so reduces the quality of life that a person wishes to die, should they be helped to do so? Life is not automatically sacred and humanists tend to support the campaign to make voluntary euthanasia legal. The word 'voluntary' is obviously very important. In fact, doctors do give terminal patients doses of pain killers which hasten the end of life, even if that is not their primary purpose. Would it not be better to legalise the situation – as in the Netherlands? There would need to be clear regulations to prevent abuse – by perverted doctors or relatives seeking gain. There might be the fear as the population profile grows older and the number of the aged needing care increases that it would be socially advantageous to administer euthanasia to reduce the demands on society. There would need to be stringent regulations with legalised voluntary euthanasia – such as more than one doctor being involved, a period of time established to ensure that the individual's desire to die was not a temporary depression, the need to ensure there is no possibility of better treatment.

Fortunately, the hospice movement (largely a Christian initiative) has improved the quality of care for the dying enormously – and this is preferable to voluntary euthanasia in many cases. Pain control has also improved. Nevertheless, many people can tell of relatives dying in uncontrollable pain and in other cases meaningless life is prolonged when an individual is in a deep coma. Suicide is a possibility available to some, but in extremity of illness this may not be possible. For those who prefer euthansia to prolonged treatment, this should be a right. The argument for voluntary euthanasia remains.

Humanists have taken a great interest in education, both as an area of moral education and as a place where religious bias remains. In Britain the legal requirement to hold an act of worship was introduced in 1944 and it was stipulated that it must be Christian in 1988 – a law which is much breached. Many head teachers and even RE teachers are not prepared to impose attendance at Christian worship on children of a very wide range of beliefs; the law remains an anomaly. Humanists have argued for RE teaching which is 'objective, fair and balanced'. This would include teaching about all religions and about humanism. There should also be some teaching of ethics, probably by studying particular social and personal problems. Local SACREs (Standing Advisory Council of Religious Education), have humanist representatives in some places. The inclusion of humanism in RE via the Agreed Syllabus Conferences has been possible.

An education which leads people to develop their curiosity and to think for themselves is obviously desirable. Teaching of morality is a difficult and sensitive area. It is more important that schools are run in a caring way and with the possibility of participation by children than that lists of rules be laid down, though without a basic level of order it is not possible to run a school (teachers at the free school Summerhill might argue that order comes from within the individual rather than from outside imposition.) Citizenship education is strongly supported by humanists. It is extremely important that morality is not tied too closely to religion, since rejection of religion can then mean rejection of morality. Humanists, as would others, wish for a high level of successful education as a means of producing a balanced society. It might be particularly important to put money into nursery education, where there is still time to offset the impoverished environment and underprivileged homes which can lead to long term social problems.

All religious groups should be entitled to run their own schools – but humanists believe they should not have financial support from the state. Currently Christians, Jews, Muslims and others are given such financial support. They must all, of course, be inspected to ensure that they give a proper education. The enormous amount of financial support given to church schools is a scandal: most such schools impose a 'Christian ethos', insist that Christian legends are true, and sometimes cream off middle class children. In some areas parents have no choice but to send their children to a church school. It must be admitted that church schools are popular – because they tend to be middle class and parents are sufficiently inconsistent as to want their children to have the religious education that they are not prepared or able to give themselves. However, far from phasing out church schools, the government is planning to increase their number and also to increase the financial support for them.

Humanists argue against religious privilege. Religious people and institutions are of course entitled to rights and there would be no case for campaigning for the complete removal of religion from people's lives. But especially now that in Britain religions consist of minority groups, there is no case for religious privilege. In fact, religious groups are arguing for a law which forbids discrimination against religions – would this lead to a stifling of the open sceptical discussion of religion?

Religious privilege remains in areas such as the House of Lords and state broadcasting. With reform of the House of Lords the statutory inclusion of bishops in the House of Lords might be enlarged to include other religions. Why should religion be a reason for a place in the House of Lords at all? (There will of course be individuals who are religious in the House, but are not there by right of their religion.)

Humanists tend to be divided as to whether to remove special privilege or to demand the inclusion of a humanist element. Should 'Thought for the Day', currently on morning radio, be abolished or should it include an occasional non-religious thought? Should RE in schools be abolished and left to parents and churches or should it be widened to include comparative religions and humanism? (It sometimes does.) Should humanists be given a place in the House of Lords?

Is reform brought about by changing individuals through persuasion and a 'change of heart', or by political action, even revolutionary action? Can education bring about more enlightened individuals or is that for the family and friends. Because the scale of humanist action is not vast, at present most humanists would argue for social change and work to bring it about through existing political means. Humanists are not Utopians and would hope to ameliorate the worst aspects of life by social action.

Another field in which humanists are active is that of providing a growing number of non-religious ceremonies. The British Humanist Association have an accredited network of officiants for non-religious funerals, weddings and affirmations, and naming ceremonies. There are also less usual ceremonies such as coming of age, divorce and scattering of ashes at sea. It is hypocritical to have a religious ceremony for someone who in no way believed in a religion.

One of the advantages of a humanist ceremony is that the programme can be tailored entirely to what is appropriate. At a funeral a personal tribute may be made, there may be poems or pieces of music, which are personally relevant; friends of the deceased may speak. And the whole event will be put in a naturalistic context – that death is part of the natural process, that biologically we cannot exist for ever, that we live on in what we have done and in the memories of those we have known. Comfort must be found for the grief-stricken: the human comfort that we can give one to another. Humanist funerals can vary from small deeply felt gatherings to big public events, if the person has played a notable part in public life. It is not uncommon for difficult and upsetting funerals for a suicide or a young child to be conducted by a humanist officiant.

It is quite possible for a family to organise and conduct a funeral in what ever way they wish without an outside officiant.

Weddings can be similarly arranged to fit the outlook of the bride and groom. Humanist weddings have taken place in unusual places, such as on a London barge or even in a diving tank (for two keen divers). Humanists also conduct affirmation ceremonies for gays and lesbians that provide an occasion for homosexuals to commit themselves to each other amid the public support of friends and relatives.

Ceremonies are occasions for humans to support each other. Is there enough done in general by humanists to sustain each other? Humanists are as likely to experience depression, marriage breakup, illness, loss of jobs, and so on, as any other group of people. There is a tendency for humanists to think in terms of autonomous individuals able to run their life in a reasonable way. Perhaps there is too much emphasis on the autonomy of the individual: we are all, to varying degrees, very dependent on the love and help we get from others. The network of humanist groups around the country can provide a certain amount of support for members in difficulty – but this is on a very small scale. The pastoral element of religion is what is most valued by many adherents. Should there be an attempt at pastoral humanism? On a small scale, maybe, yes. But it is probably best to use the existing agencies – the Citizen's Advice Bureau, the Samaritans, various counselling services : also the state welfare system can provide support. But there will never be enough, and the more humanists can do the better.

In the Netherlands and Belgium, there exist humanist counselling services. In Flanders, for instance, there is a government grant for humanistic moral counselling. An Act of Parliament states that the grant is 'to ensure that citizens who do not profess a religion may exercise the same rights to moral and ideological counselling as religious citizens and this especially in the difficult moments of life such as in times of adversity, family difficulties, sickness and death'. In Britain such counselling should be available to anyone through the secular agencies. But it could be argued that humanist counselling might provide a valuable addition.

What is particular about humanist counselling? A Flemish counsellor has written of the range of values to be found: personal autonomy, solidarity, freedom, responsibility, self-determination. These qualities sound ideal; but do they take enough account of the desperate lack of competence and contentment felt by some people?

In the Netherlands there are humanist counsellors in a variety of situations, for instance in the army: where clients are having difficulties in the military, they can be helped to cope with it, or to leave it. There are also humanists providing trauma counselling in the Netherlands.

These models cannot easily be followed in the UK, without some government funding and without a group of professional counsellors. Counselling can be extremely valuable for some people, but it is equally important to develop and disseminate ideas on ways of achieving a satisfying life.

Poker work platitudes are no use in helping people. Living life well is a craft, an art, not something which just happens. We all start from different positions, with different characteristics and differing potential. Yet for each one of us there are possibilities for achieving a satisfactory life.

Being humanist does make a difference. Our life cannot be directed to what might lie beyond this life and therefore must concentrate on what we can do here and now. We do not believe there is an overall purpose moving our life forward, and must therefore choose our own aims and ambitions. We do not believe that prayer can change anything, though reflection and meditation may be valuable in changing us or in helping us accept our situation. We do not believe that one teacher or one book is there to guide us, but we are prepared to look at the ideas of many thinkers. We do not believe that a list of commandments will assist us, for we must act sensitively in the many different situations we find ourselves and anticipate the consequences of what we do.

In his booklet 'The Humanist Himself' Harold Blackham suggests that humanism is 'a certain attitude to life'. This means 'choosing to live on the temporal terms which we can accept or refuse, and therefore assuming full and final responsibility for the life of man'. This 'is the beginning of a responsible, resourceful, self-dependent, realistic, constructive attitude to life'. If this is too much for some individuals, the social co-operation that results from such behaviour leads to assistance for all.

Self-awareness and self-understanding are of great value: to know what one can and cannot do. It is pointless to berate oneself for not doing what one cannot do. It is a recipe for disaster to be constantly unaware of ones capabilities, so that one blindly stumbles to do what one cannot and ignores the paths which may prove rewarding.

Humanists easily proclaim a too hopeful view of human nature. It can be an achievement that we do no harm as much as that we do some good. For some, daily survival is a small miracle and they can only expect the genuine but small achievements that such endurance brings about. Alan Sillitoe compared some lives to plants growing through concrete. We often cannot be sure of the outcome of our activities, even when we are attempting to do good. We may have to call on inner resources of which we are only vaguely aware. The conditions of our beginnings and our progress may be harsh indeed. There may be people who have experienced accidents or wars or natural disasters to whom we cannot easily say 'pick yourself up and rely on your resources' – although we may, in fact, be surprised at what resources people often draw upon. It cannot be stressed too much that different people are different. It is in our personal relationships with others that we find most fulfilment. The way of the recluse is not usually the way of the humanist. (Iris Murdoch wrote, in her novel *The Bell*: 'Those who hope, by retiring from the world, to earn a holiday from human frailty, in themselves and others, are usually disappointed.') Marriage may bring happiness for some, but other long-term relationships can also bring fulfilment. Ingersoll's famous comment is relevant here: 'the time to be happy is now, and the way to be happy is to make others so'.

How do humanists face sickness, death, separation, redundancy and the other traumas that people have to come to terms with? Humanism brings neither easy comfort nor false hope, which may only deceive and disappoint. We must turn to the human help that is available – often much greater than might have been expected. We are forced to call upon inner strengths that we may not have realised we possess. Instead of prayer, there is the contemplation of the things which make life worth living: a quiet walk through the park, a favourite piece of music, a purring cat, a late rose in an autumn garden, a kind gesture from a neighbour. The list can go on and would be different for each individual. Above all, for a humanist, it is the human resource that is so valuable; it is astonishing the help one person can give to another. Humanists do have ways of surviving the darker periods of life: humanism is not just a philosophy for the benign and cheerful.

Right action does not just consist of doing. To echo Tillich, 'Being is as important as becoming'. The quietist approach to life is important as well as the reforming one. The quality of attention to the world around – nature, people, art, can lead to fulfilment as well as the activities. People who have such a radiant innerness, although it is not obvious, may contribute much to others. Although humanists are not mystics, those moments of stillness, of perception of the multiplicity of the world around, can be an important part of humanist living.

Balance is a humanist virtue – it is not consistent to be a humanist and a fanatic. Most humans live below their potential, and balance and full consciousness may help in producing a rich life. Humanism may not have the full promise that all will have a good life, but as the humanist philosophy spreads there will be more fulfilment of potential and richness of human possibility.

13
The Future of Humanism

If the twentieth century can be considered an age of humanism, what lies ahead for humanism in the twenty-first century? The twentieth was a century of humanism in the sense of the drastic decline in religious belief and in the deeper sense of the growth in awareness of universal rights. As a century of war, genocide and totalitarianism it was an appalling period. As a century with the growth of the life span, reduction of disease, and increase of affluence (in some parts of the world) it may be said to have vastly improved the lot of many people.

In Western Europe there has been a catastrophic, from the churches' point of view, decline in church attendance. It is not just active affiliation to a religious group which has declined, but the likelihood of giving a religious explanation to situations and of turning to religious groups for help in life's difficulties has also diminished. This is known by sociologists as the process of secularisation, which is deemed to have taken place over the last two hundred years. Humanism is merely parasitic if it defines its progress by the decline of the churches. But humanists regard the decline of the power of religion as a definite advantage for the human species.

Positioned in one of the most irreligious countries in the world, we in Britain get a false impression. Despite the modernisation of US society, religion is a very potent force there. President Bush makes constant allusion to his 'born-again' faith and it is impossible for avowed atheists to gain political office. In this country with a high rate of church-going the influence of preachers and the so-called Moral Majority is considerable. (The US joined with traditional Muslims and Catholics in preventing a UN conference on Aids mentioning gay men and sex workers in their final statement.)

Christianity is vibrant in parts of Africa – and may soon come in its turn to send missionaries to Britain; there are already signs that the Anglican Synod is being influenced by more traditional Christians from overseas. In India, Hindu nationalism is at a high point; in the Muslim world Islam has wide social and political power. So we are not moving in the twenty-first century into a world free from religion. Indeed there may be wars of religion again: already wars in Yugoslavia and Chechenya and the Palestine-Israeli conflict have a religious dimension to them.

Can the decline of religion in the West be attributed to humanism? Probably not, certainly not by the activities of organised humanists. Nevertheless, the broad intellectual currents of scepticism, scientific materialism and humanism have played their part. However, social and economic change have been more important. Social change has removed much of the risk from life – insurance, pensions, the welfare state have led people to feel much more secure. People turn to religion to cope with uncertainty. It is the difficulty the human mind has with coping with the idea of a random universe which has led to the creation of religion. If people have the expectation of a future through to old age, of a steady income, of satisfactory accommodation, of supportive family and friends, they are less likely to turn to religion. This is not simply to opt for the bland and superficial, but to accept a substratum which gives steadiness to life.

The role of the state as a provider, a 'nanny' some would say, reduces the need for religious philanthropy. The caring for the poor and distressed will always be needed from one individual to another, but the state system ensures that most people avoid the worst excesses of poverty and disease. Influenced by the US, there has been a suggestion that some of the welfare role should revert to religious organisations (with state funding), but there is some reluctance even on the part of the churches to take this role. Such a reversal would lead to greater dependence rather than the right to independence, and there is always the risk of unwanted proselytisation. There will always be a role for humanists to support those in physical and mental distress, whether as individuals or participating in charitable organisation. And perhaps this is a way in which some meaning can be found in life. But the essential point is that security and affluence in the modern world have made religious groups redundant. It could be argued that material needs are only part of the human requirement and that attending to people's emotional, intellectual and aesthetic needs are equally important. Did the beauty of medieval cathedrals compensate for the poverty and depression that the poor Christians of the time experienced? Probably not. The religious may criticise the humanists for laying emphasis on material well-being, but life without is pretty paltry.

Religion is surviving more in the emotional than the theological sphere and more in the area of individual choice than as social obligation. Private illumination counts for more than public argument. (See J.C.A. Gaskin, *The Quest for Eternity: an outline of the philosophy of religion*) In that sense religion is now more humanistic. Although fundamentalist Christianity is alive and well, especially among evangelicals, there are now quasi-humanist currents in groups such as the Sea of Faith and individuals such as the former Bishop

Holloway, who has written a book expounding the humanist point that it is possible to have morality without God.

Cults and sects, some harmless, some sinister, appeal more to the young than to traditional churchgoers. Humanism may be more easily undermined by New Age philosophies than actual cults which are followed by very few. New Age notions such as meditating on the vibrations of the universe or getting closer to trees, might be attractive to some but they abandon reason and science. In some cases, such as Scientology, a sect has gained much wider support. No doubt there will be other new religions in the future. A religion is usually a cult that has gained long-term acceptability. Despite the decline of Christianity in the West, it seems unlikely that religion will wither away – and humanists will settle for a pluralist society, with a neutral state, and tolerance of a wide range of beliefs.

If humanism is well grounded as a belief system it should be relevant to the world as a whole. Will humanism fall on stony ground in other continents than Europe? There is little sign of humanism developing in Africa, in Asia there are nodes of humanism that might grow, in the US atheists are regarded as Satanic. It is hard to be optimistic, but the influence of bodies such as the United Nations, even if lamentably weak, in promulgating human rights might help the growth of a humanist outlook. It is necessary to develop a humanism that speaks to the oppressed and the insecure.

To be a humanist it is not enough to be non-religious – and if humanism is to survive it must reach out with a moral sense, which is partly biological and partly the exercise of the free choices that lie before us. Even in irreligious countries such as Britain, humanism does not have a firm hold: nihilism, hedonism and confusion are more wide spread.

Although the nurture/nature arguments about individual development are swinging back to the 'nature' axis, with research on genetics, the humanist emphasis on the education of the individual will not lose importance. Education will not really help until it becomes much more than a system of training children to jump through hoops. The development of creativity, independence and originality of thought might help. The Internet is bringing in possibilities of individual learning that may prove very fruitful. Communication by e-mail and mobile phones becomes rapid – but what is being communicated? Perhaps a microchip in the brain will bring permanent contact between people – which at least will mean that those who do not want to listen to the conversation of others on mobile phones will not need to!

The future may be entirely other than we expect. At the beginning of the twentieth century no one expected war on the scale of the First World War. At the same time manure from horses drawing carriages was thought likely to be a serious problem in the future. Then came the motor car .... And other problems! We can imagine vastly spiralling technology – the microchip linked to the body, the development of clean energy, the lengthening of the life span, the list could spiral into fantasy, but when the changes of the last century are considered, it becomes certain that there will be wide and unexpected new developments. Humanism has a pragmatic approach, constant principles, but adaptation to altered circumstances should enable survival. It may be said that religions can be very adaptable too – Christianity would not have survived 2000 years without enormous adaptability.

An alternative scenario posits a civilisation moving backwards. We may have to face the kind of change considered in the chapter on environment. Climate change will lead to the rise of sea levels threatening low lying populations, may revive diseases such as malaria and tuberculosis (in parts of the world at present not affected) or bring new diseases (as happened with AIDS), may bring loss of habitat and food through drought and flooding. The consequence of this may be water and food wars, mass migrations, destruction of the world's economic system. Such devastating change would lead to social unrest and the disappearance of political systems. How would humanism fare in such a future? There might be social confusion and insecurity which would lead people to turn more to religion; there might be unreason in the face of the fear which would accompany such a change. It would be the role of humanism to remain a voice of reason, looking at the situation rationally, seeking rational solutions. It might become a still small voice in the face of colossal disorder.

I think humanism will survive whatever the changes. It may become more or less effective, louder or quieter. I suspect throughout recorded history scepticism has always been there: it is visible during the classical period of Greek philosophy, it is only seen during the Middle Ages as, say, the cheeky gargoyles protruding from some churches, it is there in the poetry of Omar Khayamm. A moral component to life will always be needed in the future no less than the past. Religions may not disappear, but their dominant and oppressive elements can be contested. The influence of the Renaissance and the Enlightenment will not easily be lost – however challenged by post-modernists. (I predict post-modernism will be long forgotten, when the ideas of the Enlightenment remain potent.)

Humanism is not simply a bundle of campaigns. Humanism will only survive if it attends to the whole person. Beyond our daily concerns, most of us have a sense of the infinite and the eternal, however much our beliefs may be profoundly human. Humanism is a philosophy that can appeal to all, that can give us the hope that we may act constructively in the future and live richly in the present.

Appendix 1

Amsterdam Declaration

This is a statement of humanist beliefs agreed at the International Humanist and Ethical Union at its 50th anniversary conference in the Netherlands in 2002.

1. **Humanism is ethical.** It affirms the worth, dignity and autonomy of the individual and the right of every human being to the greatest possible freedom compatible with the rights of others. Humanists have a duty of care to all of humanity including future generations. Humanists believe that morality is an intrinsic part of human nature based on understanding and a concern for others, needing no external sanction.

2. **Humanism is rational.** It seeks to use science creatively, not destructively. Humanists believe that the solutions to the world's problems lie in human thought and action rather than divine intervention. Humanism advocates the application of the methods of science and free inquiry to the problems of human welfare. But humanists also believe that the application of science and technology must be tempered by human values. Science gives us the means but human values must propose the ends.

3. **Humanism supports democracy and human rights.** Humanism aims at the fullest possible development of every human being. It holds that democracy and human development are matters of rights. The principles of democracy and human rights can be applied to many human relationships and are not restricted to methods of government.

4. **Humanism insists that personal liberty must be combined with social responsibility.** Humanism ventures to build a world on the idea of the free person responsible to society, and recognises our dependence on and responsibility for the natural world. Humanism is undogmatic, imposing no creed upon its adherents. It is thus committed to education free from indoctrination.

5. **Humanism is a response to the widespread demand for an alternative to dogmatic religion.** The world's major religions claim to be based on revelations fixed for all time, and many seek to impose their world-views on all of humanity. Humanism recognises that reliable knowledge of the world and ourselves arises through a continuing process of observation, evaluation and revision.

6. **Humanism values artistic creativity and imagination and recognises the transforming power of art.** Humanism affirms the importance of literature, music, and the visual and performing arts for personal development and fulfilment.

7. **Humanism is a lifestance aiming at the maximum possible fulfilment through the cultivation of ethical and creative living and offers an ethical and rational means of addressing the challenges of our times.** Humanism can be a way of life for everyone everywhere.

Index